The Northern Lights

The Northern Lights

BY

GEORGE FRASER

AND

KEN PETERS

HAMISH HAMILTON

LONDON

First published in Great Britain 1978
by Hamish Hamilton Ltd
90 Great Russell Street London WC1B 3PT
Copyright © 1978 by Aberdeen Journals Ltd

British Library Cataloguing in Publication Data
Fraser, George
    The northern lights.
    1. Press and journal   2. Evening express
    I. Title   II. Peters, Ken
    079'.412'35   PN5139.A/
    ISBN 0-241-10073-9

Printed in Great Britain by
Western Printing Services Ltd, Bristol

Illustrations

Composing machines being loaded for transportation to Mastrick

Then Secretary of State for Scotland, Gordon Campbell accompanies Lord Provost James Lamond, Lord Thomson of Fleet and Mr. K. J. Peters on the opening day at Mastrick

The Queen Mother's visit to Mastrick

Sir John Betjeman, the Poet Laureate, unveiling a plaque to commemorate Alexander Cruden

The Rt. Hon. Bruce Millan, Secretary of State for Scotland, studies typesetting by computerised photocomposition in 1978 in the *Aberdeen Journal*'s composing-room

The giant press room of Aberdeen Journals' new plant at Lang Stracht, Mastrick

Pipers and drummers of the 51st Highland Volunteers at the little Normandy seaport of St. Valéry-en-Caux beside the Highland Division memorial

William Veitch, editor-in-chief from 1927–57

Lord Thomson of Fleet with K. J. Peters

Press and Journal editors in the 1950s, 1960s and 1970s: George E. Ley Smith (1950–56) and James C. Grant (1960–75)

Peter Watson, the present editor appointed in 1975

Evening Express editors: George Fraser (1944–53), Robert Anderson (1956–59), H. R. Bawden (1959–62), Robert Smith, the present editor appointed in 1962

Chapter 1

The year is 1748. It is Wednesday, the fifth day of January. From a hand-operated press an excited printer removes the first copy of a newspaper destined to make history. True, it is not much of a publication compared with the size and concept of the newspapers of the latter half of the twentieth century, but it is a beginning and a beginning to something that is still with us.

It is not difficult to envisage the scene and to conjure up the atmosphere as James Chalmers, second son of Dr. James Chalmers, of the Chair of Divinity at Marischal College, Aberdeen, stood by to witness the birth of his brain child. He had trained himself well for the day and the hour, but even he, as he stood there, although he must have hoped for great things, could not possibly have foreseen that No. 1 of *The Aberdeen's Journal*, as he named it, was about to start a sequence that would span well over a couple of centuries and thrive today as *The Press and Journal*, the oldest surviving newspaper in the whole of Scotland.

Of that he could not have dreamed, but it is fair to assume that his mind did hark back to the exciting days when he made his first attempts to issue broadsheets from the same office. Particularly in his mind must have been the occasion when Jacobite forces occupied the town in the autumn of 1745, after Johnny Cope had embarked his troops and sailed for the Forth and ultimate defeat at Prestonpans.

Always a Royalist, James Chalmers must have, somehow or other, aroused the wrath of the Jacobites—probably by the issue of a none-too-complimentary broadsheet. At any rate, a party of Prince Charles' followers raided his office. An entry in a diary by the Rev. John Bisset, a minister in the city, dated 22 November, gives some idea of what took place:

> Poor Chalmers, the printer, is from home, not yet able to walk with his strained leg he got jumping a window to escape the ruffians . . . They have committed great outrages in his house, breaking open an outer door when not let in, setting fire to an inner door, and, when let in, scattering his types, searching his house, burning papers and breaking presses and drawers.

This happened, it was indicated, eight days before the date of the diary entry.

Another account describes how, after leaping from the window, Chalmers made his way towards the Bridge of Dee (Don?) where he sought shelter in an outhouse only to discover that it was full of Jacobites.

Unaware of his identity, they treated him kindly, but it must have come as a bit of a shock to be asked, 'What's that—Chalmers, the printer doing now?' Happily he had the presence of mind to reply that he was still printing Royalist manifestos, an answer that made some of the clansmen drop to their knees and swear, with drawn dirks, that, if they laid hands on him, they would have his blood. It is idle to speculate as to what would have happened to James Chalmers and to the history of journalism in Aberdeen and the north if these fiery Jacobites had realised who their companion really was. In the event James Chalmers must have been very glad to get away, and the story has it that he ultimately found refuge in the home of a King's College professor.

A later entry in the Rev. John Bisset's diary would seem to lend credence to the belief that Chalmers had published some sort of anti-Jacobite broadsheet. In this the diarist gives vent to his fear that 'we will see no more of his news schedules'. That, on the face of it, seems to be the correct version of the sacking of the printing office. The diarist's date rules out another account which postpones the incident until after the defeat of the Jacobites at Culloden on 16 April 1746.

It has been claimed that two days after this crushing blow to the Jacobite cause, there emerged from James Chalmers' printing-press a broadsheet giving a full account—an eyewitness account—of the battle. It was this report, according to the second version, that enraged Jacobite soldiers retreating from the fateful field of Drumossie, via Aberdeen, and led to the sabotage already described. But this version is discredited by the fact that it is more than doubtful whether any Jacobites did, in fact, retreat by way of Aberdeen.

Be that as it may, there seems to be little doubt that James Chalmers did suffer from espousing the Hanover cause. He himself, according to his grandson, served with the Duke of Cumberland's Army at Culloden and it would not be too far fetched to suggest that, if he did not actually write the eyewitness account, he at least arranged for its despatch.

History has many strange twists. It is a matter of interest that among James Chalmers' adversaries in those days were the great-great-grandfathers of Mackenzie King, who, as Prime Minister of Canada, recalled two centuries later, how these two grandfathers of his mother's father, William Lyon Mackenzie, fought in the 'Forty-Five as followers of Bonnie Prince Charlie. What would have been Chalmers' reflections had he been able to foresee that a distinguished Canadian descendant of these two Jacobites would be congratulating the paper on its two-hundredth year of existence as Prime Minister King did on 5 January 1948?

Back to that despatch. In our era of high-speed telegraphy, wireless and television two days seem a long time for it to get into print at Aberdeen, but it should be remembered that, when Culloden was fought, the fastest means of travel and communication was the horse. In point of fact, to report the tidings so soon was a feat comparable with that which brought the good news from Ghent to Aix or of Waterloo to London.

Unfortunately no copy of that famous issue seems to have survived, although it is just possible that one could be hidden away among old papers in more or less forgotten archives. In fact, there was a suggestion that one was in the possession of the Rev. James Smith, one time schoolmaster at Ballater; but the Rev. John G. Michie, who had been his assistant, wrote

3

in the *Journal* in 1895 that he had never seen the sheet and that a subsequent examination of Smith's papers, which had been given to various parties, failed to disclose any such copy.

And what of the newspaper itself? Whatever plans James Chalmers may have had for its regular issue seem to have been forced aside at least temporarily, by the demands of his army duties and of his appointment as official receiver on certain Aberdeenshire estates forfeited as a result of the Rising.

But even during this period he was to provide evidence of where his heart really lay. Whatever the Jacobites may have thought, James Chalmers was a man of peace, and while he waited to get back to the job he really wanted to do, he was responsible for the issue of a number of bulletins in which the constant plea was for the restoration of tranquillity.

Like the 'Culloden newspaper', these bulletins seem to have failed to become collectors' pieces. But here again it is just possible that one day an original copy will be found.

James Chalmers, as has been indicated, prepared himself well for newspaper proprietorship and production. A man 'well skilled in the learned languages'—he demonstrated that fact again and again in the columns of his newspaper—he brought also a practical vein to his task. There was a time when he seemed to be destined for the Church and that appears to have been the purpose for which he was sent to Oxford University. In the event this proved to be a turning-point in his life, for it was while he was there that he was introduced to, and became fascinated with, the art of printing.

His subsequent move to the House of Watts, in London, the leading printers of the day, was almost inevitable for a man of James Chalmers' imagination and enterprise. One of those tales that somehow gain currency and become more and more established by repetition is that Benjamin Franklin was his colleague and friend while he was there. Unfortunately the time factor is all against this possibility and that false link must, at some time or other, have been forged by a too fertile imagination.

In 1736 James Chalmers returned to Aberdeen well versed in the art of printing, to set up a printing press of his own in what was then a new building, the property of the Corporation and sited on the north side of Castle Street, as it was then called —Union Street was a dream yet to be dreamt, let alone fulfilled.

With tenancy of those buildings went the title of Official Printer to the City and the University of Aberdeen. It helped him to achieve the prosperity that enabled him to woo and marry Susannah Trail, daughter of the Rev. James Trail, minister of Montrose. And it was when he was thus established that he set about the publication of *The Aberdeen's Journal and North British Magazine*.

As we have seen, he must have felt that army and official duties had kept him away far too long from his printer's desk, but, rid at last of these ties, he was soon picking up the threads of his business again and planning anew, in less turbulent times, the launching of the newspaper that was to make journalistic history. And such history! A hundred years later Lord Provost Thomson was to hold up a copy of No. 1 of *The Aberdeen's Journal* at a dinner, held in the County Buildings, in celebration of the centenary of the newspaper's production and say: 'I trust that this venerable document will be preserved for many generations and that it will surprise, gratify and delight the company which may perchance assemble one hundred years hence to celebrate the second centenary as we are celebrating the first.' Well, such a company did assemble—in the Music Hall on 5 January 1948. The folio number of *The Press and Journal* on that day was 29,019. Shades of No. 1.

It was an occasion for many tributes, best symbolised perhaps by that paid by the Marquess of Aberdeen: 'It is because *The Press and Journal* has kept on giving the north-east people,' he said, 'what they have wanted over the 200 years that have passed without a distinct change of the character of the paper that it has lasted these two centuries. It started well and it has continued well.'

The reference by Lord Provost Thomson, a hundred years earlier, to the possibility of such a bi-centenary gathering did not pass unnoticed. It was William Veitch, Editor-in-Chief, who reminded the gathering of it and, in turn, looked ahead a further hundred years, to a third such assembly, wondering what the nature of the speeches would be then.

'One thing I do know,' he added, 'the speakers will not be talking about the manual labour required to print the sheet as it was 200 years ago. They will not speak about the steam power used to produce the papers 100 years ago, nor will they talk about the electric power by which the paper is produced today.'

He was speaking at the dawn of the Atomic Age and saw in it a pathway to vast changes in the methods of newspaper production.

From 1748 then down to the present day, through ten reigns, *The Aberdeen's Journal*, though it has changed its name more than once, has continuously recorded the passing scene. Its pages have reflected the vast changes in the national way of life as they happened, and particularly as they affected the area it has served so long. They have recorded the transformation that has taken place in industry and the great advances time and human endeavour have wrought in the economic, social, educational, religious and medical spheres. One can trace in its columns agricultural developments from the primitive methods obtaining when the newspaper first saw the light of day—in stock breeding, in crop rotation, in the quality of the crops themselves, in the plough, in mechanical appliances and, in recent years, in the almost complete disappearance of the horse. The Industrial Revolution in which Britain led the world is seen against a background of labour troubles, marked by the Chartist movement, leading to the birth and development of the trade unions. Particularly noted in this connection was the threat the new methods of production provided to the old rural crafts which meant so much to the north-east and the Highlands.

Recorded, too, with not a little justifiable wonderment, are the giant strides made in the fields of transport and communications—the digging of the Port Elphinstone to Aberdeen canal which, incidentally, brought lime to the farms and increased crops to the city, the construction of the railways, the introduction of the motor car, the realisation of the age-long dream when man began to fly, first by heated balloon and then in heavier-than-air, power-driven machines. The story of the advance of communications is no less exciting. In the files are to be found reports of the first efforts at telegraphy, of the introduction of the telephone, of the triumphs of Marconi, of the advent of broadcasting, of the discoveries of Baird, the Scot who put the world on the way to the triumph of television.

There are tales too of the sea, of the old windjammers, the *Thermopylae* the pride of them all—at any rate as far as the north-east was concerned. A new era is indicated as the first crossing of the Atlantic is made through a combination of sail and steam and the Australian wool and the China tea runs begin to shed something of their glamour.

Changing days, changing ways! The surge of time and thought and ambition is reflected, too, in the birth of the steam trawling industry, in engineering triumphs exemplified throughout the area by bridge and harbour construction or reconstruction, in the ups and downs of the granite industry, in the success of the paper-making and the tweed mills.

In these yellowing pages is to be found also the story of the great educational strides that succeeding generations contrived to make—the union of King's College and Marischal College, the spread of the secondary school movement and, generally, the forward-looking policy and practice that was to put the northern half of Scotland in the very forefront of educational standards and progress.

Alas, it has fallen to the newspaper's lot to record as well, again and again, the fact and consequence of man's inability, or unwillingness, to settle international disputes in ways other than that of the grim arbitrament of arms.

Culloden, it is true, was the last battle to be fought on British soil—if we discount the Battle of Britain which was, of course, engaged in *over* British soil and the waters that wash our shores. Not that we haven't been threatened with such battles. Twice in the lifetime of the newspaper has invasion seemed imminent.

In the year of its Jubilee (1798) it was reported that Napoleon was preparing thirty huge, unsinkable and incombustible rafts, each to carry 10,000 men across the English Channel. On

7

these rafts were cannon and furnaces to heat the cannon-balls red hot so as to keep our fleet at bay. It is history that, as with Napoleon's plans of invasion, so it was with Hitler's plans in World War II. Each was an unfulfilled dream.

But, if Britain contrived to keep the peace within her confines and to scare off possible invaders, her sons have all too often been called upon to fight and to die on foreign fields. Many pages have been stained at least figuratively with the blood of those men who went forth to war, so many of them to return maimed, so many never to return at all. There must have been many days in the history of the paper when its arrival in north-east homes was awaited in fear lest it should be the bearer of grim tidings of personal loss.

In sunshine and in shadow then, in days of good fortune and ill, the *Journal* has been faithful to its trust as recorder of contemporary event and thought and aspiration, as the vehicle, too, for individual opinion and for guidance where such was indicated or sought.

Such is the background against which the newspaper, down the years, has had its being. It has lived on because, throughout its history, it has sought to be accurate with its news, to be loyal to the community it serves, to have standards of taste second to none.

Chapter 2

The stage is set. It is time we had a closer look at Act 1, Scene 1 —at No. 1, as it was described on the title page of *The Aberdeen's Journal*. On this page, too, was the statement that it covered the news 'from Tuesday, 29 December 1747, to Tuesday, 5 January 1748', a declaration that signified the founder's intention to publish his new paper once weekly. And once weekly it continued to be published for 128 years, until 25 August 1876, when it became a daily newspaper.

On the back page was the following imprint:

Printed and sold by James Chalmers, and by Alexander Thomson, Bookseller. Subscriptions and Advertisements are taken in by James Leiper Merchant, Alexander Thomson Bookseller and James Chalmers Printer. Postages paid by the Publisher. (Price Two Pence).

It will be noted that punctuation in those days did not exactly follow modern practice and that the printers of the period were generous in the use of capital letters. Let it be added here and now, however, that the English is almost invariably a pleasure to read.

The invitation to advertisers is interesting. In point of fact only one had availed himself of the opportunity afforded by this new venture, an indication, surely, of the short-sightedness of Aberdeen's business men of the day. The appearance of *The Aberdeen's Journal* must have presented a rare opportunity for shopkeepers at least to inform customers of what was new in their wares. It must have caused no little stir in the city, small though it was then with its 9,000 inhabitants living in less than a score of streets.

One anonymous writer, looking back from the vantage-point of the closing years of the nineteenth century and, no doubt, making use of various contemporary authorities, has described its nature and contours as follows:

Aberdeen was bounded on the east by Justice Street, on the south by the Trinity Burn and the Quay. Small even as this area was, nearly one half of it was occupied by the Churchyards of St. Nicholas and Trinity, St. Katherine's Hill and many pleasant 'gardings and orchards adjoyning', now covered by the foul and festering tenements of Exchequer Row and Shiprow...

The Castlegate was the main thoroughfare of the burgh; while the Broadgate, then built only on one side, took rank as the second thoroughfare in importance.

The Denburn flowed peacefully to the sea, while between it and Guestrow there was much swampy ground that gradually merged in the wild fastnesses of the liberties of the Stocket and anon joined hands with primeval bog and heather.

For the most part the houses were built of wood with 'stake and rice' chimneys, the streets were narrow and dirty, and, if some authorities are to be believed, open middens not infrequently saluted the nostrils of the passer-by, while the domestic pig on occasions fought for possession of the King's highway.

No. 1 made its bow then to a small, not so salubrious city. It was a single-sheet production, folded over to give four pages, measuring about 14 inches by 9 inches and divided into three columns.

No. 1 gave no local news, but that was to be remedied in the third and subsequent issues. It contented itself with reproduction of what the Editor considered to be the most important and the most interesting news items printed in the London papers.

First is recorded the havoc wrought among shipping off the Flanders coast by a gale. Then follows news from The Hague that the Princess of Orange is seven months gone with child.

Farther on, a sidelight is provided on the war being waged with 'the Crown of Spain and the French King'. It takes the shape of a condemnation of what looked like an effort to sell 400,000 quarters of wheat to France which, presumably, would have been a profitable transaction in view of the report, also printed, that 'the mob have rose on the Magistrate of Toulon on account of the great scarcity of corn.'

Editors in those days had little to fear from the laws of libel and could be pretty free with their opinions.

That there were versifiers around even in those days is indicated by the reproduction of a jingle bemoaning the incidence of new taxes. If the writer had but known what the *Journal* readers of over two centuries later would have to suffer from Chancellors of the Exchequer. . . .

However, no doubt the poet of the hour considered the situation, as he knew it, bad enough in all conscience. He headed his effort 'No More Gambols' and lamented:

'Twas merry at Christmas when Money was Plenty
And *Taxes* took off not above *Five* in *Twenty*:
But how is it possible *Mirth* should arise
Now *all* that can *make it* is under *Excise*,
When *Light* is *not free* in the worst of *dull Weather*?
Wheels pay, if *we ride*; if we *foot* it *shoe-leather*!

Alas, to every era its trials and tribulations!

In these days of hydrogen and atomic bombs is it any consolation to be reminded that there were men in 1748 exercising, as now, their minds with thoughts of a bigger bang? It is reported:

They write from Paris, that the Apothecary who was to have made an experiment of a new kind of Gun-powder, in the presence of Marshal Saxe, having employed a person to dry a quantity of it for that purpose, by some Accident or other, it took Fire and blew up the Operator and the House, and did considerable Damage in the Neighbourhood.

No doubt operators were expendable in those days—as they sometimes seem to be in ours.

The sole advertisement, already referred to, suggests that somebody was prepared to compound a felony. It is printed in italics and reads:

That on the 29th of last Month were amissing three promissory Notes of the Aberdeen Company, one for 1ol and two for 20s each, and of the Bank of Scotland, two for 20s. Whoever brings them to the publisher of the paper, shall have two Guineas reward and no Questions asked.

Were that to appear today a lot of questions would be asked!

Be that as it may, the publisher of No. 1 must have realised full well the commercial need to encourage advertisers to use his columns. The charges he set down as ' 2s. 6d for the first time, and 2s for each time afterwards.'

His appeal did not go unanswered. The trickle that followed soon began to take on the character of a stream, itself to broaden until, a half-century later, a writer in *Chambers' Journal* was to describe the Aberdeen paper as the most lucrative concern in Scotland, distinguished alike for the number and for the high class of its advertisements.

No. 1 concludes with a message to the reading public. It states:

Those who are so good as to encourage this Undertaking may transmit their Names and Places of Abode; if in Town, the Paper shall be carefully sent to their Houses by twelve o'clock on the Day of Publishing; and to those in the Country, by the first Post or Carrier.

The Price from the Post Office, 10s a year.

It was the beginning of a newspaper that was to grow in power and influence with every passing year: it was the beginning, too, of a delivery service which, though it has changed and improved in many other ways, has so developed its postal distribution that, in this respect, it is second to none throughout the length and breadth of the land.

Considerable space has been devoted to No. 1. No apologies are offered, for, after all, it does represent a successful beginning, and that means probably more in the launching of a newspaper than with any other commercial enterprise. It opened the door for James Chalmers and *The Aberdeen's Journal*. One might almost say that it swung it wide open.

Exciting days lay ahead for James Chalmers with moments of high adventure a month or so after publication of the first issue.

The story goes that he had occasion to go to London. Travelling by sea, he had the misfortune, with his fellow passengers, to fall into the hands of a French privateer. However, after five days of captivity on board the Frenchman, they were returned, minus their trunks and contents, to their ship which duly reached London. At least, as a good newspaperman, he had the satisfaction of securing a real 'scoop' thus early in his journalistic career.

There is an overwhelming temptation to linger over the early issues of *The Aberdeen's Journal*—incidentally, the 's' was soon dropped to provide the more euphonious title of *The Aberdeen Journal*.

There is an amusing picture of the 'disaster' to the dandies of the town when a great storm scattered the wigs of 'such citizens as were necessarily abroad' and deposited them in the neighbouring fields. We are reminded, too, that the barbers of those days were just as ready as their prototypes today to find excuses for raising their prices. There is an advertisement which reads:

Taking under consideration that for several years past the expense of living has been greatly increasing, while there has been no alteration in the prices for their work, the society (the Society of Barbers and Wigmakers in Aberdeen who, incidentally, pulled teeth and let blood over and above their tonsorial duties) beg leave to inform their customers and the public that they find it necessary to raise the rates for their work from and after the first day of April next. They have, at the same time, resolved the addition shall be so moderate that they hope their customers and the public will not consider it unreasonable.

Be it said for those barbers of yesterday that they did, at least, present their case with some elegance.

That there were delinquents about in those days is clear. What is even more evident is the grim manner in which authority dealt with them.

On 10 May 1748, John Davidson, an Angus man and a deserter from the English Army after the Battle of Fontenoy, was charged with 'sorning and housebreaking.' He was sentenced to be executed at the 'crossing of the roads on the lands of Rudriston and the Bridge of Dee and thereafter to be hung in chains.'

In another case it would appear that Alexander Cheyne, from Fyvie, made the mistake of his life when, having been outlawed for 'nocturnal theft', he voluntarily attended to prove his innocence, only to be found guilty and be sentenced to be hanged in the Market Place on 8 July. And a pretty grim job, too, were those hangings. The *Journal*'s own reporter describes how another wrongdoer, Alexander Phillip,

> was brought down to the Court in his grave linen, with cap and gloves tied with blew ribbon. When he came to the gibbet the minister prayed with him; he sang some part of the psalms from the Psalm Book; and when he was about to be turned off declared to the crowd as he should answer to his Maker that he had only robbed or stolen. He acknowledged that he was due money to some people, but that many of the spectators were more in debt than he.

There may have been a lot of truth in what he said, but, unfortunately for him he was the one the law had caught up with—at any rate for the time being.

And so one turns the pages—to learn of cattle stealing at Aberdeen, of sheep stealing at Kintore, of the fact that the Litster's House at Mill of Bourtie, for some years a place well employed for business in dyeing, waulking and dressing cloth, is to let, of a thirty-three-year-old looking for a wife with £100 to her name, of a swarm of locusts at Peterhead and of the excitement created by the appearance of a comet.

Always there is the impression of James Chalmers hard at

work behind the scenes, putting the imprint of his character on his paper. Occasionally he was to give expression to his ideals in more direct form. As in the New Year message he wrote in verse for his readers as his paper drew to the close of its first year of publication:

> My grateful thanks for all your favours past
> Which pray continue this year as the last.
> From every post impartial I will cull
> Whatever is not trifling, false or dull;
> And though no more you must expect to hear
> Of cities stormed or castles blown in air
> The fruits of peace, of concord and of joy
> And happier events shall the press employ.

The year, it should be explained, had seen an end to the war with France and the signing of the Peace of Aix-la-Chapelle. Alas for James Chalmers' hopes, the respite was to be short. The beginning of the Seven Years' War was but eight years away.

With two years of success behind him he was again to wish his readers the compliments of the season. In the files one can read:

> Two years have now passed since the paper was first published and, as it has always been my study to avoid giving offence to any person or party, the crying demand for it flatters me of its kindly reception by the public who now have an opportunity of being served with the most material occurrences, foreign and domestic, of the whole week at an easy rate. If in mistake some paragraph appears from what may be called a party paper, let it be considered that there is a difference between author and publisher, that the liberty of the press shows us to be a free people, and has often been found a check upon those in power; and sometimes complaints without doors have had a very happy influence on councils within.

James Chalmers was quite a man, with very definite views about the freedom and the purpose of the Press. Two years later he was to have his journalistic ability put to the supreme test by the appearance of opposition.

In January 1752, the *Aberdeen Intelligencer* was launched by Messrs. Douglas and Munro, but *The Aberdeen Journal* was too well established, too popular to be shaken. Nevertheless, James Chalmers decided to give his readers a still better bargain. He introduced new type 'of a smaller size which means it contains more matter.' It might be added that his old type 'faces' were pretty well worn out by this time!

The battle did not last long. February 22, 1757, saw the last of the *Intelligencer*. It was swallowed up by the *Journal*, a procedure that was to become something of a habit with that newspaper as the years rolled by. It is of interest to note that a copy of the *Intelligencer* was presented to Aberdeen Public Library in 1928 by a local teacher. It was believed to be the only surviving issue of that paper. It covers the period 'Tuesday, July 30, to Tuesday, August 6, 1754'.

Slowly and surely James Chalmers, that man of vision, built on the sound foundations he had laid. But he was not to escape entirely the pitfalls inseparable from newspaper publication. It was the custom of the day for any offending publication to suffer the indignity of being publicly burned at the hands of the common hangman. Such was the fate, on one occasion, of *The Aberdeen Journal*.

The trouble arose over an action taken against James Smith, saddler and late Convener of Trades, for having stated publicly that Alexander Livingstone, of Countesswells, and former Provost of Aberdeen, was largely responsible for the high price of meal in 1752. For the record, James Smith was found guilty, but sentence was delayed so that he could attend at the bar and beg Alexander Livingstone's pardon. This he did and that was all there was to it.

Chalmers made ample apology in the following terms:

What was inserted in this paper of the 23rd. inst., as publisher of *The Aberdeen Journal*, I hereby acknowledge was rash and indiscreet for me in publishing and printing the same, and I hereby declare that I am now satisfied that what was inserted with respect to the usage of the meal retailers by the rioters was a false representation of the true facts; and that the paper given and printed by me in the paper of the ninth inst. was an untrue account of the affair between Provost Livingstone and J. Smith and printed by me in the *Journal* of the twenty-third current, which was, by sentence of the magistrates yesterday, publicly burned by the hands of the common hangman.

It was a rare fall from grace, not to be repeated by Chalmers. Indeed, there does not seem to be any other record of the paper having to suffer the fate of that particular issue, not at the hands of the public hangman, at any rate.

Chapter 3

For sixteen years James Chalmers presided over the destiny of the paper he had launched and steered towards prosperity. When he died on 25 August 1764, he was succeeded by his eldest son, James, then only twenty-three and learning the business of printing in London. His was to be a long and eventful innings. James Chalmers the Second had studied at Marischal College and at Cambridge University. To his father's business he brought a penetrating mind and a knowledge of the arts as well as of printing, qualities that were to serve him well during the remaining forty-six years of his life and of proprietorship.

At the age of twenty-eight he married Margaret, daughter of David Douglas, Laidas, a member of the Tilquhilly family, a fruitful union, as it proved to be.

His reign was to be marked by two important visits to the city by outstanding literary men of the day. Robert Burns himself noted in his diary what transpired when, in 1787, in the course of his tour of the North of Scotland, he came to Aberdeen.

> Came to Aberdeen—met with Mr Chalmers, printer, a facetious fellow—Mr Ross, a fine fellow, like Professor Tytler—Mr Marshall, one of the poetae minores—Mr Shireffs, author of 'Jamie and Bess', a little decrepit body with some abilities—Bishop Skinner, a non-juror, son of the author of 'Tullochgorum', a man whose mild and venerable manner is the most marked of any in so young a man—Aberdeen, a lazy town.

The meeting with the bishop actually took place in *The*

Aberdeen Journal printing office where an hour's conversation covered a wide variety of topics. That the author of *Tullochgorum* was very happy about this meeting between his son and Burns is clear from the epistle he wrote to the bard later. It begins:

> O happy hour for every mair
> That led my chil' up Cha'mers' stair;
> And gae him what he values sair,
>   Sae braw a skance
> Of Ayrshire's dainty poet there,
>   By lucky chance.

The other visitor to the city was Dr. Samuel Johnson, accompanied, of course, by his biographer, Boswell. It would seem that Dr. Johnson had not, by then, made the same impact on the North of Scotland as he had done on London. At any rate, on 6 September 1773, the *Journal* merely recorded: 'A few days ago arrived at this place Dr. Samuel Johnson, author of the English Dictionary, Rambler, Idler, Ec., together with James Boswell, Esq., of Auchinleck.' And that was all. One wonders how greatly Dr. Johnson's vanity was hurt by this simple dismissal of his presence—that is to say if he ever saw the report.

There is an amusing record elsewhere, descriptive of Dr. Johnson's 'blind peregrinations through the town, feeling his way at every lamppost.' He is said to have come into violent contact with a workman who was harling the side of a house in the Broadgate.

'Sir,' Dr. Johnson is reported to have said, 'I trust that the impact of my person did not incommode your labour.'

To which the workman, never stopping his splashing, is said to have answered: 'Na, na, sir; if ye're nae in yer ain wye, ye're nae in mine.'

And that seems to have reduced even the redoubtable Dr. Johnson to silence.

That Chalmers' mind was continually exploring publication possibilities in other directions is evidenced by the issue in 1771 and from time to time after that, of the *Aberdeen Almanack*, a sort of precursor to the *Aberdeen Directory* as we know it today. Tucked away in odd corners there may well be copies of the early issues of the *Almanack* just as there are copies of eighteenth-century *Journals*. Lord Tweedsmuir, for instance, has a complete file, at Potterton House, of the latter from 1757 to 1762. He often turns over the pages of these old *Journals* which were given to him by a friend who bought them at a farm roup in the north-east. As for the *Almanack*, its authoritative standing can well be gauged from the fact that Burns wrote to Gavin Hamilton on 7 December 1786: 'I am in a fair way of becoming as eminent as Thomas à Kempis or John Bunyan, and you may expect to see henceforth my birthday inserted in *Aberdeen Almanack*.'

The second James Chalmers was not to escape, any more than his father, the test of competition. John Boyle, in 1770, made a bold attempt to publish a rival journal, but *The Aberdeen Journal* was too well established by then to be shaken and the threat was of short duration.

Chalmers himself, with the same urge as his father's to extend his publishing activities, conceived the idea of launching the *Northern Gazette and Literary Chronicle and Review of the Month*. His plan was to reproduce extracts from the best contemporary authors, a sort of 'Literary Digest' of its day. Unlike *The Aberdeen Journal*, however, it did not prosper and the last number was issued within a year of its birth.

As to *The Aberdeen Journal* itself, the files show that this James Chalmers did not believe in leaving matters as they were. On 3 October 1791, he changed publication day from Tuesday to Monday. At the same time he divided the pages into four instead of three columns and the price was increased to 3½d. Round about this time, too, the progenitor of the leading article began to appear.

Another milestone in the life of the *Journal*, as well as in that of James Chalmers the Second, was the flitting of its presses to a building behind the Town House, to premises originally erected for a ribbon factory. That happened two years before the close of the century. It was a move that was scarcely worth the trouble, for, in 1813, the removers were in again and the business was shifted, lock, stock and barrel, to Adelphi Court. That was three years after James Chalmers the Second had departed this life.

During his proprietorship he had seen many local developments, and perhaps the most interesting for us nowadays is the opening of the Aberdeen-Port Elphinstone Canal, on 31 May 1805. No doubt he was there at the inauguration ceremony. At any rate his newspaper reported:

> We have now the pleasure to report the opening of the Aberdeenshire Canal. On Friday morning the Committee of Management assembled at the Basin at Inverury and embarked on board one of the barges, The Countess of Kintore, and sailed through the canal to Aberdeen.

It went on to say:

> The canal passes about nineteen miles into the interior of the county, rising 170 feet above the level of the basin at Aberdeen by means of seventeen locks; is 3½ feet deep and 20 feet broad at surface water. One barge has already delivered a cargo of coals at Inverury and another 85 bolls of shell lime at Kintore.

The latter reference to lime is an indication that the farmers of the north-east were well aware by this time of the value of that commodity in the cultivation of the soil.

In his later years James Chalmers the Second was to see the construction of Union Street, the first steam engine erected in the north-east and the launching of some of the great Telford bridge building and harbour construction enterprises in the area. He died on 17 June 1810, leaving the fortunes of *The Aberdeen Journal* in the hands of his second son, David, then only twenty-two years of age and destined, like his father, to a long reign—forty-four years, to be exact. Like his father, too, and his grandfather before that, he was to leave his own imprint on the paper as well as in aspects of life in the city.

James Chalmers the Second was buried in St. Nicholas Churchyard where the curious may still read, on the table stone that marks his last resting-place that he 'left to his numerous offspring a bright example of every social and every Christian virtue.'

There is a graphic history on that selfsame stone, that goes on to record the death, on 14 August 1818, of his beloved wife; of their son, David, on 24 April 1859, and of his wife, Ann Lamb Campbell, on 20 March 1870; of David's eldest son, James Chalmers, on 10 March 1895, and of his wife, Theresa Isabel Brander, on 19 June 1906; of David Montagu Alexander Chalmers on 31 July 1929, and of May, eldest daughter of David Chalmers of Westburn and widow of Thomas Arnold, London, on 18 May 1894.

Before we pass from James Chalmers to his son David it is fitting to note that he left behind two other memorials to himself and his regime, memorials which seem to be as permanent as that kirkyard table stone. The first is the grandfather clock which he bought, round about 1769, from James Abercromby, five times Deacon of the Hammermen in Aberdeen, and set up as a constant reminder to his staff on the fleeting character of time and of the need in a newspaper office for punctuality. Having reached its bicentenary of service, this fine old clock, an unfailing timekeeper, stood guard for a few years more over the movements of the men in the caseroom but has now found an honoured place in retirement, a reminder of the days that were and an object to be pointed out with veneration to new-comers and to visitors who may pass that way.

The veteran clock was referred to in the *Journal* of 21 May 1894, on the occasion of the firm's removal from Adelphi Court to Broad Street. Its description then as being of 'superior workmanship' was well deserved as its long life, before and after this flitting, has amply proved. A further reference to it was made by the late James A. C. Coutts, then general manager, in the issue of *The Press and Journal* of 24 March 1925. He, too, paid tribute. It was 'still going strong', he wrote, 'keeping time with wonted accuracy' and he considered it 'good for a long spell of life, being made of hard and well-tempered material.'

It didn't let him down.

The other memorial is the press on which, five years after

James Chalmers' death, was printed the stirring news of the Duke of Wellington's victory over Napoleon at Waterloo.

The news was conveyed to Aberdeen and the north-east by means of a single-sheet special edition, issued on Sunday, 25 June 1815. A framed fragmented copy of this bulletin hangs today on one of the walls of the editorial sanctum of *The Press and Journal*. It reads:

Aberdeen Journal Office,
Sunday, June 25, 1815.
Most Important
Intelligence
Just Received from the Lord Provost of Edin-
burgh, (now in London and transmitted by
express to Aberdeen)
London, Thursday, 22nd . . . past One in the
Morning.

Major Percy, son of Lord Beverley, has just arrived with the account of the greatest VICTORY ever known, obtained by The Duke of Wellington, near Charleroi. The French attacked his Grace's Position on Sunday, 18th at Day-light and they . . . Attack and be Repulsed the whole day.

. . . Evening, the Duke began generally to Charge and drove . . . them before him, and obtained the completest victory ever heard of.

The result is THREE EAGLES, now at Carlton House, and ONE HUNDRED AND FIFTY PIECES OF CANNON taken by the British Army under the Immortal Wellington.

GENERAL BULOW, in his Pursuit, took SIXTY Pieces more.

A Day so contested and so ended, been obtained, as may be supposed, by immense Loss.

I can give you no names yet, not having seen the return. Thank God, LORD WELLINGTON is safe. It is not true as formerly reported, that GENERAL PACK is killed. That there has been the Hardest Fighting is already known in Edinburgh and I should not send these tidings by express,

23

but as the feeling of those who have near relations with the Army must be on the stretch, I cannot resist gratifying the Inhabitants of the Good Town and its neighbourhood with the most Important Communication that ever CAME TO BRITAIN.

City Chambers, Noon, 24th June, 1815.

Today that sturdy press is a showpiece in the hallway of the new building on the Lang Stracht. The engineers who constructed it must have vied with the clockmakers of their day in building for posterity as well as for the hour. Generation after generation of caseroom apprentices had, before its retirement, tugged at those handles, if not with the enthusiasm of the pioneers, at least with due regard to the legibility of the product as demanded by a whole succession of overseers less durable than the machine.

Chapter 4

The way is clear then for a survey of the David Chalmers regime, except perhaps to explain why it was that he, the second son, should have found himself at the helm.

It so happened that his elder brother had sought his fortune elsewhere. He had set up a printing press at Dundee and it was in the family tradition that he should play an important part in the launching of the *Dundee Advertiser*. In January 1801, Dr. Stewart, one of Dundee's leading surgeons, whose project it was, asked James Chalmers to do the printing for him. James himself had, in fact, tried, two years earlier, to establish the *Dundee Daily Mail*. Apart from that, it was the experience the printer had had with his father in Aberdeen that induced Dr. Stewart to give him the contract. For the first few months of its existence the *Advertiser* bore the name of James Chalmers on its imprint and he was paid 30/- for each weekly issue. In October 1801, however, it was announced that Chalmers was giving up the work because it was his intention, owing to 'some recent unforeseen circumstances to reside in another part of the country'.

David Chalmers brought to his task, if not experience, at least all the enthusiasm of youth, laced with a keen intelligence and the integrity which had been a marked characteristic of his predecessors. At the very outset he had the spur of competition to test him out. The *Aberdeen Chronicle* had been launched four years earlier and, later on, there were to be the additional challenges of the *Aberdeen Observer* (1829) and the *Aberdeen Herald* (1832), the latter taking the place of the *Chronicle*.

In the case of the *Herald* the word 'challenge' seems to be an apt one, for there was an occasion in the thirties when James Adam, the portly Editor of the *Herald* challenged David Chalmers of the *Journal* to a duel on the Links, but it would seem that better counsels prevailed, and the duel never took place.

With the advent of the *Herald* David Chalmers was not slow to make the claims of the *Journal* known. In the issue of 22 August 1832, he declared:

> To our Readers
>
> In pursuance of a resolution of the House of Commons, there was lately laid before Parliament a table of the number of stamps issued to, and the sum of advertisement duty paid by, each of the newspapers published in Scotland. This table has been in circulation for some time, but we have delayed transferring it to our columns until we should be able to accompany its publication by a substantial mark of that gratitude and pride with which we cannot but regard the fact that the document in question places us at the head of the Scottish newspaper press in point of circulation.

David Chalmers went on to describe the form in which he had decided to mark his 'gratitude and pride'.

> We this day (he wrote) present to the readers of the *Journal* our weekly sheet, of a size far beyond that of any newspaper that has yet appeared on this side of the Tweed—in point of typographical accuracy and arrangement second to none and, we trust, not inferior to any in the extent, the variety or the interest of its contents.

Circulation figures, of course, speak louder than any words of self-praise however much the speaker may be entitled to use them. The Parliamentary figures could not be more illuminating. They were:

Aberdeen Journal	2231
Edinburgh Weekly Journal	2192
Scotsman	1914
Glasgow Herald	1615

26

James Chalmers, the
founder and first editor

Robert Burns meets the Editor of the *Journal*, James Chalmers (son
of the founder, extreme right) and Bishop Skinner in the office of the
Aberdeen Journal in 1787

The grandfather clock in the Production Department. Installed in 1769, it was on duty when Robert Burns first visited the office

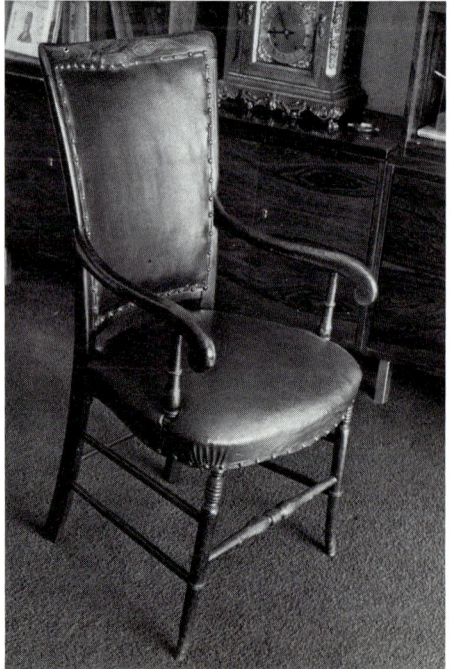

Baillie Chalmers' chair dates from the 1830s and is still in the managing director's office

The *Free Press* clock now in its third home and approaching its centenary

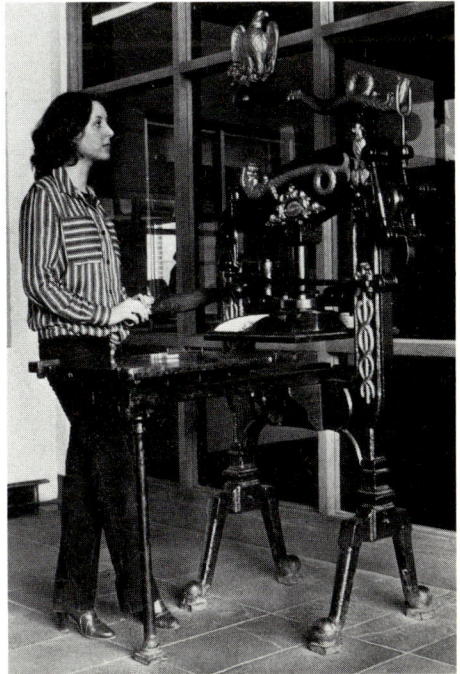

A special edition of the *Journal* after the Battle of Waterloo was printed on the famous Eagle proofing press which stands today in the office foyer and has been in the firm for nearly 200 years

Offices old and new: (*left*) the Free Press building in Union Street, Aberdeen, in 1900, and (*below*) after the amalgamation of the two local newspaper companies in Broad Street— a scene in the 1920s or 1930s

The reporters' room in the 1920s

Women have always played a big part in the work of Aberdeen Journals Ltd.
Here they are seen in the composing-room in the 1920s

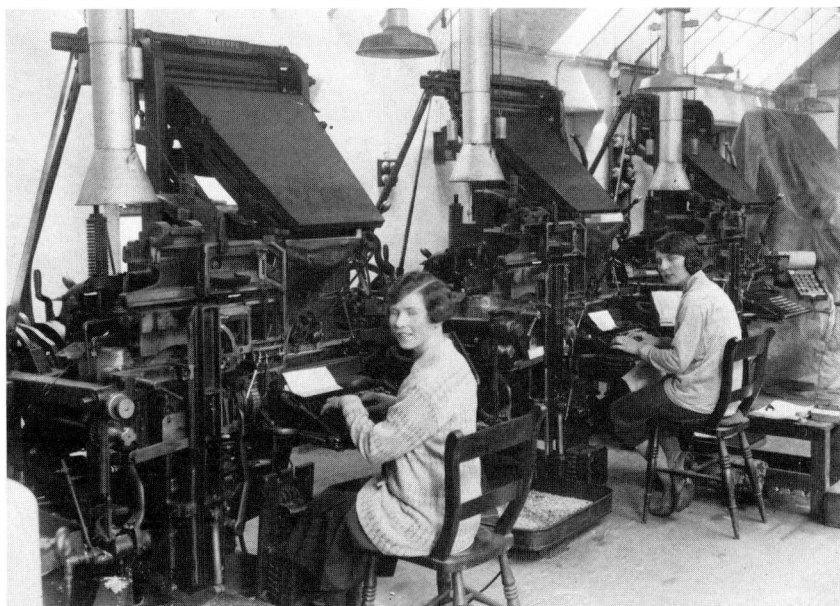

Speeding the papers to the doorsteps . . . by horse and trap

by motor vans

by aircraft to Orkney and Shetland

by rail

Administrative and accounting offices in the 1920s
and the 1960s

Edinburgh Evening Courant 1603
Dumfries Courier 1452
Dundee Advertiser 1163
Inverness Courier 615
Perth Advertiser 596
Aberdeen Observer 404
Dundee Courier 250
Elgin Courier 250

It will be seen that the circulation of the *Journal* was considerably greater than those of the *Scotsman* and the *Glasgow Herald*, a situation that still obtains today. But circulation figures, then as now, are not a complete guide to actual readership. There is plenty of evidence that the issues in David Chalmers' days passed from hand to hand and many more people than those who actually purchased them became aware of their contents.

Later figures show that sales mounted steadily under his guidance, stimulated particularly by the repeal of the Stamp Act in 1855, which sent all newspaper sales rocketing. As a matter of interest it might be pointed out here that, in 1885, an auditor's certificate gave the daily printing of the *Journal* and *Express* combined as 20,318 copies. The calculation was based on the period from 31 January to 30 April.

The *Journal*'s progress, it should be further pointed out, was made despite the experience of challenges from rivals other than those listed. In 1837 the *Aberdeen Constitutional* made its bow, to be followed, five years later, by the *Aberdeen Banner*. In 1853 came the greatest challenge of all—the launching of the *Aberdeen Free Press* as successor to the *North of Scotland Gazette*.

It is worthy of note that not in circulation alone was the *Journal* supreme in those testing days. The claim has been made, and seems to have been substantiated, that no other newspaper in Scotland carried as many advertisements.

So much then for readership and advertising, but these did not represent the total sum of David Chalmers' achievement. He was to set the pace, too, in the technical field of newspaper

27

production. He was the first in Scotland to introduce the steam-driven printing press. That was in 1830. By that time the manual presses must have been hard put to it to meet the growing readership demands.

During his regime the first centenary celebrations of the *Journal*, already referred to, were observed. How high he himself was held in regard in Aberdeen—he had served several terms on the Town Council—and in the counties is made evident by the fact that some 200 leading figures in the area entertained him at dinner. Presiding was Lord Provost Thomson and among those present were the Principal and Professors of the University, the Baillies and Town Councillors, representatives of the Society of Advocates, leading traders and manufacturers and many county gentlemen. Reference has already been made to speeches made on that occasion. Worth adding might be Barclay of Knockleith's remark that he had, as a worthy neighbour in his parish, a centenarian who was four years older than the *Journal*.

It transpired that this grand old man, despite his great age, had intended to be present at the function, but 'a bit o' a cauld' made him change his mind. To him is attributed the description of the first issue of the *Journal* as being 'jist like twa leaves o' my Bible.'

One more contribution to the life and progress of the *Journal* for which David Chalmers was responsible remains to be recorded. This was the introduction of the leading article, at first casually and later regularly, which involved the definite appointment of an assistant who was also to be leader-writer.

First to occupy this post around 1830 was a Mr. Weir who came from the south. Later he was to join the *Glasgow Herald*, to be succeeded on the *Journal* by John Ramsay, wit and poet and great conversationalist.

Of the two, John Ramsay undoubtedly left the greater impression. He was one of a gifted coterie of local poets, wits and antiquarians who brought the city into the limelight as a centre of literature and the arts. Among them were Joseph Robertson, James Adam, Robert Brown, William Duncan and Thomas Spark. None was of sprightlier mind than John

Ramsay. One particular shaft of his led to his portrait being painted.

He was attending a public dinner in the days when black velvet vests were very much the fashion. John Ramsay did not conform and the fact drew a succession of gibes from an unmannerly medical 'gentleman', but even he was silenced when Ramsay retorted, 'Doctor, the mort cloth is not the insignia of my profession.'

'Ramsay, I'll paint your portrait for that hit,' said the well known artist, James Giles, R.S.A. And he was as good as his word.

John Ramsay was born in London in 1799, the only child of a ship-master who traded to the West Indies. When John was nine, his mother, a Blairdaff woman, returned to Aberdeen where John went to the Grammar School, while his maternal grandmother saw to his religious and moral training and saw to it well.

The bold wit that was in him got an early airing when his mother, after he had said the Lord's Prayer, asked him to add something of his own—something he wished God to grant him. On bended knee and to his mother's shocked amazement, the youngster promptly invoked: 'Oh Lord, gie my mither a better temper; mak' her —'. And that was as far as he got; for such was the 'dirl in the lug' which followed that, sixty years later, when telling the story, he said it was still ringing.

John, somewhat older and wiser, proceeded, in 1813, to King's College as second bursar, graduating M.A. four years later. Like the first James Chalmers, he had been intended for the Church, but he turned to private teaching until the post of private secretary to Joseph Hume, M.P. for Montrose Burghs, was offered to him. This, however, did not appeal to him and he returned to Aberdeen about 1830 to become a teacher at Gordon's Hospital. During his four years there he became a contributor to *Blackwood's Magazine*, the *Aberdeen Magazine* and other periodicals before he began his connection with the *Journal* which was to last for fourteen years.

John Ramsay had many interests over and above his literary ones which made him the friend of Wordsworth, Miss Mitford,

Joanna Baillie and Lord Aberdeen. He was a fine mathematician, although he failed to secure the Chair of Mathematics at King's College when it fell vacant in 1851. He was a keen antiquarian, becoming a member of the Cambrian Archaeological Association, and he was skilled in campanology, a skill he exercised often in the belfry of St. Nicholas Church.

A biographer has said that these bells were among the last of John Ramsay's earthly thoughts. Just before he died, in June 1870, he was heard to whisper, 'These bells are not right placed.'

William Forsyth, who succeeded him as leader-writer, and eventually became the first Editor of the *Journal* other than a Chalmers, was born in 1818, at Turriff, the son of a watchmaker. After attending the parish schools of Fordyce and Turriff he went to Aberdeen University for a session or two before going on to Edinburgh to study medicine.

In 1838 he returned home to Turriff to become assistant to Dr. Shand. Of an adventurous nature, he twice went on whaling trips to the Arctic as medical officer, after which he returned to Edinburgh to continue his studies. An attack of jaundice, however, compelled him to return home and it was during convalescence that he took to writing—and discovered his real bent.

After a short period of journalistic work on the *Inverness Courier*, in 1843 Forsyth became sub-editor on the *Aberdeen Herald*. His writing so appealed to David Chalmers that, when John Ramsay's health broke down in 1848, the *Journal* proprietor induced the *Herald* man to flit from Queen Street to the Adelphi, to a career that was to bring him to the very top of his profession.

William Forsyth had the great virtue of being a practical man as well as a poet. As leader-writer, he wrote with punch and character. The leisurely life of a leader-writer on a weekly newspaper suited him. We shall meet him again in the hurly-burly of editorship of a daily newspaper, a more hectic existence which was less to his liking.

David Chalmers' long reign as proprietor and guiding spirit of the *Journal* came to an active end in 1854 when he made over the management to his two sons, James and John Gray Chalmers. He had seen the birth of the *Free Press* and no doubt the onerous duties created by strong competition induced him to shed the load five years before his death.

To his sons was to fall the biggest decision of all, except perhaps that of the first James Chalmers when he founded the paper. But their hour of decision was not to come till May 1876, and in the interval they carried on their task with conspicuous success.

Apart from the development of the *Free Press*, first in 1865, from a weekly to a bi-weekly publication, and then to a daily newspaper in 1872, the greatest factor in the life of the *Journal* during the James and John G. Chalmers regime was the emergence of the Great North of Scotland Railway system which revolutionised methods of delivery. Furthermore, it was a time of national crisis, first with the Crimean War to be waged and, hard on its heels, the shock of the Indian Mutiny.

Nearer home, and of great interest to a local newspaper, big events were reported. In 1855 Balmoral Castle was completed. And here a word of warning to reporters in general may not be out of place. There's no knowing when their sins will find them out and, worse still, the trouble they may cause to future generations of their kind. When the foundation stone of the Great Tower at Balmoral was laid the ceremony was described in the *Journal* of Wednesday, 5 October 1853. In the report the future home of Queen Victoria was described as a palace and it was this description that led to an inquiry, made by the Editor of *The Press and Journal*, on behalf of King George VI, in 1948, as to when Balmoral ceased to be called a palace. The conclusion was ultimately drawn that the reporter had over-reached himself and that, in fact, the castle had never been a palace.

But to return to the record of great local 'occurrences' as they were called in those days. In 1857 Queen Victoria opened the new bridge at the Linn of Dee and Captain McClintock sailed from Aberdeen on the Fox in search of the Franklin Expedition. In 1860 came the union of King's College and Marischal College with the University of Aberdeen, and, three years later, the new Grammar School buildings were opened. Exciting, too, was the first appearance (in 1869) of velocipedes in Aberdeen and, no less wonderful, the first traction engine or road steamer, as it was sometimes called. In 1871 Aberdeen's new Town House was opened, the city boundaries were extended and Victoria Park was laid out.

These are but some of the events that loomed large in the life of the north-east and in that of the *Journal* while James and John G. Chalmers were at the helm. And all the time it was gaining in readership and in popularity and not in the city alone. Incidentally, none knew that better than the printers who had to fold by hand, at a rate of between 600 and 700 an hour, all the papers as they came off the machine.

How eagerly the *Journal* was awaited in the country districts is well exemplified by a letter sent to the Editor by the Rev. J. G. Michie, Dinnet. The reverend gentleman had forwarded to an old friend of his in Canada a copy of the *Journal* surveying its life-story just as it was embarking upon its 150th year. It was this friend's letter of thanks that the minister sent to the Editor.

My first impressions of the *Journal* (he wrote) are connected with the Crimean War. On my way home with the *Journal* I remember being called in from the road by James Robertson, restoring old James Roy's house after the fire which had occurred some time previously, who eagerly seized the precious paper and devoured the war news, reading to himself aloud.

On reaching home, my father met me and asked if the war had begun. I replied I did not know, but there had been some shooting anyway.

We were nearer the Post Office than the rest of the club and therefore our family had the first look of the paper. After us it did service in no less than six homes, each successively having its use for one whole day.

I can well remember my poor father sitting in the chimney corner under the double shell cruisie lamp, reading for the good of the whole household the interesting news from far and near. During the exciting time of the war the other members of the club could not await their turn, but eagerly sought the light of the great luminary in the house of the first in order.

I can yet hear the voices as the story of scenes of heroism and death were recited from the *Journal*'s pages. As they rose to applaud some action in which 'oor folk' drove all before them, and again, as scenes of carnage were depicted, I can hear my mother's almost tearful 'Poor fellows!'

Then the talk would go on about the war, the stories of old campaigns were in order, for 'Boney' and his wars were a very live subject to the fathers of that day.

Next day the *Journal* would find its way to Loanhead to meet, no doubt, a like reception there, and thence, in turn, to Bogarieve, Pitellachie and the two Knocksouls. On its journey it would be lighted by whale oil, candles and fir roots, but in no house on that route would it see a lamp that would be sufficient to give light to the eyes of the present generation.

Remember that was written in 1897; and it refers to a period over forty years previously. The light may have been poor. At least the *Journal* saw to it that these good neighbours did not go unenlightened.

Chapter 5

James Chalmers, like the founder, had done part of his printer's training in London before starting up in business in Aberdeen. His brother, John, graduated M.A. at Marischal College and did a great deal for charity and education. His memory is perpetuated by a stained glass window in the West Church of St. Nicholas and by his Chair of English Literature at the University of Aberdeen to found and endow which he left £10,000.

As has been indicated, the brothers were very much in the throes of competition from the very start and these circumstances obtained as long as they retained sole proprietorship of the *Journal*. The *Aberdeen Free Press*, as it developed to its daily-issue status, naturally was the chief rival, but another newcomer in the field, the first evening newspaper in Aberdeen —the *North Star*—was also to give pause for thought.

How much this mounting rivalry had to do with the ultimate decision to accept the purchase offer of a company, formed in February 1876, is anybody's guess, but at least the new firm, with, it is true, much more ambitious plans, had a pretty rough road to travel before prosperity was attained.

These plans and purposes were perhaps best defined by the late Colonel Innes of Learney, eighteen years after the event, when he spoke at a ceremony to mark the removal of the firm's seat of operation from Adelphi Court to Broad Street. As he himself then said, he was 'intimately connected with the inception and foundation of the Company'. 'In the year 1866,' he went on, 'the Conservative Party encountered a disastrous reverse, after a long period of success, by the defeat of Sir James Elphinstone by Mr Dingwall Fordyce, and we who were interested in the Conservative Party at that time could not help thinking that our want of success was largely due to the lack of backing by a daily print. Well, Mr Patrick Chalmers (of Messrs. C. and P. H. Chalmers and a grandson of the second James Chalmers) an active soul in the business, and I thought it would be possible to organise a company to set up a daily paper. We entered into communication with Mr Westcombe, the proprietor of the *Edinburgh Courant* and various other newspapers, and held a good deal of correspondence with him, but the great difficulty was this: so far as the Conservatives were concerned the ground was occupied by an old-established and successful weekly, *The Aberdeen Journal.*

'*The Aberdeen Journal* was proud of its position and rather scorned to adopt a party advocacy. We could not therefore find the possibility of clearing the ground and the enterprise was dropped.

'For the next eight years we brooded over our disappointment. I come next to 1874, when we obtained the services of a candidate, upon the division of the county into two, in the person of Mr Edward Ross. Our object was to rouse the party, and we did excite a certain amount of interest, and we took up again the question of a daily paper. But we were again unsuccessful.

'The next question I am to refer to is one which, more or less, concerns myself. Upon the retirement of Mr McCombie I came forward as candidate for West Aberdeenshire. I had no desire to enter Parliament, but I had a very strong impression of the desirability of endeavouring to rouse the party in the county. In eleven days I went over the county and appeared at forty-one different places and made forty-one different speeches, and although I was defeated, a considerable interest was evoked in the party and this was kept up by an arrangement, prompted by me, whereby Messrs. Chalmers published a daily broadsheet.

'Following upon this, capital was subscribed and the influential weekly *Journal* was taken over from the Messrs Chalmers.'

That's the story as Colonel Innes told it. It can be supplemented from the Minute Books all of which have been preserved.

From Minute Book No. 1 it can be gathered that the first meeting of the Aberdeen and North of Scotland Newspaper and Printing Company (Limited), as it was called, was held on 2 March 1876. The company had been registered on 28 February. At that meeting, it is recorded, William Yeats of Auquharney was elected Chairman, with Alexander Davidson of Desswood, Aberdeen, Vice-Chairman, both offices to be held until the first General Meeting of the shareholders. Appointed as additional Directors and on the same basis were Colonel Innes of Learney, William Black Ferguson (Aberdeen), William Ferguson of Kinmundy, Dean of Guild Walker (Aberdeen), James and John Gray Chalmers (the late proprietors), James Badenoch Nicolson of Arthur House, Henry Wolrige-Gordon of Hallhead and Esslemont and Thomas Balmer, Gordon Castle, Fochabers. Patrick H. Chalmers was appointed interim secretary.

The first the general public knew of the change in ownership was when they read, in the issue of the *Journal* for 17 May 1876, an announcement, itself dated 15 May, to the following effect:

> The proprietors of the *Journal* have to announce that they have disposed of the copyright of *The Aberdeen Journal* newspaper and the Goodwill of the Printing and Publishing Business to The Aberdeen and North of Scotland Newspaper and Printing Company (Limited) and that, for the future, the *Journal* will be published and the Printing Business conducted by the New Company under the management of Mr John Thomson.

The new owners announced in the same issue that the business would be continued in all its branches and, further, that they were making arrangements to publish the *Journal* daily while continuing to publish a weekly issue.

The John Thomson referred to had held a similar appointment on the *Bradford Chronicle and Mail*. Subsequently William Forsyth was confirmed in his position as Editor, with control over the 'tone, taste and selection of the literary part of the paper', and he was further instructed to 'remain in the office nightly till he could fairly leave the remains of the preparation for the morning's issue in the hands of the assistant-editor.' The latter post was offered to, and accepted by, William Gillies.

The interim Directors, Chairman and Vice-Chairman got the blessing they needed, at the first General Meeting (27 June) of the shareholders. The proposal to issue the *Journal* daily as soon as possible was approved, the Directors were confirmed in their office and James Augustus Sinclair, C.A. (later to become the Earl of Caithness) was appointed auditor.

The road was clear for the launching of *The Aberdeen Journal* as a daily newspaper and, in bringing this about, the Directors made it clear that, while the weekly edition was to be continued, the daily issue was a direct continuation of *The Aberdeen's Journal* founded in 1748. In the weekly issue of 23 August 1876, a notice was printed to the effect that:

The ABERDEEN AND NORTH OF SCOTLAND NEWSPAPER AND PRINTING COMPANY LIMITED, having acquired the Copyright of the ABERDEEN JOURNAL, so long and favourably known in the North-Eastern Counties, have pleasure in intimating that the JOURNAL will be PUBLISHED as a DAILY MORNING NEWSPAPER on and after FRIDAY, the 25th August current. . . .

Having outlined the policy of the daily issue, the statement continued:

The Weekly Edition of *The Aberdeen Journal* will be published every Wednesday Morning, as heretofore, but on and after Wednesday, the 30th day of August, the paper will be considerably increased in size and reduced in price from Twopence to One Penny per Copy.

This statement should dispose of all doubt as to what the Directors had in mind. They never had any other idea than that, while they were directing the flow into two channels, the wells of origin for both were the same. On 25 August then, with the 6,712th issue, the *Journal* became a daily newspaper, with the same high hopes as those that had marked its foundation 128 years earlier.

We trust (declared the new proprietors) that, by God's blessing, the *Journal* may work, day by day, and all its days, with fidelity and an honest purpose to good ends.

The need for daily publication was emphasised in a leading-article which looked to the 'past, present and future'.

A weekly newspaper (it propounded) must, necessarily, fall more or less out of harmony with the currents of daily thought and action. History is treading on our heels; and the transient records of journalism, to do their proper work, must breathe the living breadth and dramatic interest of the day in the same way as they present an all but hourly index of the fluctuation of the markets.

It was in William Forsyth's best vein.

It would have been too much to expect, however, that there would be no teething troubles. They came all right, and not only on the economic front. It has already been suggested in this survey that William Forsyth was less suited to the hustle of daily publication than he was to weekly journalism, and it is perhaps not surprising that, in February of the following year, an arrangement should be made that he would ultimately give up the editorship.

But by November, in the same year, it was the management that was under fire, and it was decided then to abolish the position of general manager and to ask William Gillies to add those duties to his own as assistant editor while William Forsyth carried on as Editor. It was round about this time, too, that Colonel Innes succeeded William Yeats as Chairman of Directors.

If the *Free Press* challenge had been considerable during the Chalmers' reign, it was nothing to what followed when the *Journal* daily edition really got under way; and we find Forsyth pressing the Directors with the need to do something in response to the fact that his rival was regularly issuing eight-page papers against the *Journal*'s four pages. He was calling for a bolder policy. It would seem, however, that the response was not to his mind. At any rate, he resigned on 1 February 1879. The probability is that the Directors were, at the time, much more concerned with plans to 'turn out a halfpenny paper to be called the *Evening Express*'.

But before we permit the intellectual William Forsyth to slip quietly into the shadows, if only to prove that no man is perfect, let's record one last characteristic of his. He had probably the worst handwriting of all to occupy the *Journal* editorial chair. There is, in fact, an entry in the Minutes of the Acting Board of Directors, under the date of 30 August 1878, to the effect that the 'Managing Editor was directed to consult Forsyth as to the extra charge by compositors for setting up his MS.' Those were the days when 'comps' worked on piece-rates and 'bad copy' undoubtedly slowed down output and reduced earnings. There is a story that one 'comp', completely stumped by Forsyth's calligraphy, returned it to the Editor who had to confess that he could make nothing of it himself and had to bestir his memory to recall and to rewrite what he had in mind. Another story, apocryphal perhaps, but often associated with Forsyth, has a 'comp' suggesting that, if given his fiddle, he might be able to play his otherwise illegible 'take'.

Be that as it may, one can at least sympathise with Gillies in his task of tackling, in his managerial capacity, his senior on the editorial side. It must have called for diplomacy of the highest order. That, Gillies may or may not have had, but the fact remains that he had to report that he had not succeeded in making any arrangements with Forsyth and he was further instructed by the Acting Committee to 'report the matter for disposal by the Directors at their General Meeting.'

Alas, there is no record in the Minutes of the ultimate 'disposal' of the thorny problem and, in any case, Forsyth's departure from the scene was perhaps the only effective solution.

Chapter 6

Reference has already been made to the Directors' concentration on the launching of the *Evening Express*. One might have expected a flood of publicity in advance of this journalistic plunge, but that was not the way they did things in those days. Publicity was to be a child of the twentieth century, and that was some way off yet.

Their plans completed, the Directors were content to make the following announcement in the *Journal* of Saturday, 18 January 1879:

On and after Monday, 20th. January,
will be published
Aberdeen Evening Express,
a first-class local newspaper with
telegraphic general and commercial news
to hour of publication.
Price one halfpenny

This announcement was repeated in the *Journal* on the day of publication. And that was that! The *Express* was left to sink or swim. And, as we know, it is still very much afloat.

The *Evening Express* was, in fact, lucky with its day of publication. Perhaps it would be fairer to say that the Directors saw to it that it was launched, purposely, on the day the trial began of the Directors of the Glasgow Bank, a trial that was on everybody's lips. News was coming to hand, too, of the end of General Roberts's famous march from Kabul to Kandahar.

Nearer home, there was an event which caused great rejoicing at Methlick and at Tarland. From 37 Grosvenor Square, London, came news that the Countess of Aberdeen (of

'We Twa' fame) had been safely delivered of a son and heir.
As the Methlick correspondent put it,

When the news arrived a merry peal was rung on the parish bells and flags were hoisted at the Post Office and the Registrar's Office. In the evening a quantity of fireworks was set off at the North of Scotland Bank, and, while I telegraph, the village is illuminated in grand style. Everyone seems delighted and the village band, in full force, is making the night musical. The cannon at Haddo House have been fired at intervals during the evening.

The *Express* made an immediate impact, and it is on record that the demand for the first issue was such that the printing machines could not cope with it. For the record, the issue consisted of four pages of six columns each.

It would be interesting to learn whether there are still copies around of Number 1 of the *Evening Express*. If a touch of spleen may be permitted the writer, it would be directed at the vandal who ripped Number 1 from the first bound file in the publishers' possession and so marred an otherwise complete record. Maledictions upon him, live or dead!

Whose idea was it to launch the *Evening Express*? It may or may not have been the child of any one brain, but it is perhaps worth noting that, when the newspaper was celebrating its Jubilee, Dallas Ross claimed that it was Gillies' idea. Ross was in a fairly good position to make the point as he took over the editorship of the paper from Gillies soon after it was launched. One thing somebody did see to, and that was to emphasise the up-to-date nature of the news. Paragraph after paragraph was sub-headed 'This Day'. This applied particularly to court cases. It was a practice adhered to for quite a number of years.

It is time to pick up again the threads of the *Journal* story. It will be recalled that Forsyth's resignation followed his expressed dissatisfaction with the prospects of having to compete, on a size basis, with the *Free Press*. Perhaps he was a bit hasty in his reaction, for it would appear that his pleas for a larger *Journal* did not fall entirely upon deaf ears. At any rate, on 4 July 1879, the Acting Committee agreed to eight-page issues for at least three days of the week, and by the end of the year the manager had been instructed to order a two-feeder printing-machine.

But over the next few years it was still a hand-to-mouth existence. Lack of sufficient capital had been the handicap from the start and a real crisis was reached in 1884 when it was decided to go into liquidation and to reconstitute the Company. This accomplished, the new Board met on 2 May and unanimously elected Garden A. Duff as Chairman, with Alexander Walker as Vice-Chairman. Patrick H. Chalmers having been made a Director, the secretarial duties were undertaken by Messrs C. and P. H. Chalmers. As it transpired, this work fell on the shoulders of D. M. A. Chalmers ('Monty' to his friends), son of James Chalmers, and he it was who eventually proved to be the last of the long line of the Chalmers family to be directly connnected with the working of the firm.

James Augustus Sinclair, who acted as liquidator of the old Company, was retained as auditor and, with Gillies seeking pastures new, Charles Macaskie was appointed to succeed him as manager and Editor, a post he was not to hold for very long. In November 1886, he and the firm parted company following a dispute over newsprint, but in his short reign he had seen the *Journal* pass yet another milestone. On 26 September 1884, it was decided to produce regularly an eight-page *Journal*.

With Macaskie's departure, the Directors appointed George Esson manager of the Commercial Department and a Mr. Gray (chief sub-editor) head of the Literary Department, as they called the Editorial Department in those days. Esson had had long associations with the Company in its various forms. He had first entered the office in 1849, in the days of David Chalmers. To begin with he had served his apprenticeship as a typographer. At the end of 1861 he went to London where he had training in commercial and managerial work. Domestic considerations brought him back to Aberdeen in 1876, and it was the Chalmers family who paved the way for his return to his first love. To his appointment as manager, when it came, was added, a few weeks later, that of Editor when Gray tendered his resignation because of ill-health.

Esson was soon to discover that his job was to be no sinecure.

The financial clouds which had darkened the horizon ever since the Company had been formed were not yet to lift and, by 1888, the Directors were considering the possibility of dropping the *Journal* altogether. Before them was a memorandum, based on figures supplied by the manager, showing that there would be a profit on the *Express* and the *Weekly Journal* and the other branches of the business were the *Daily Journal* discontinued. Happily the suggestion was rejected, and steps were taken to raise locally the sum necessary to ensure continued publication. It was round about this time that a number of employees helped out by purchasing Debentures and a Staff Committee was formed to make suggestions.

This same year of 1886 produced a misfortune of which journalists on the staff today get constant reminders—and none, he makes bold to say, more keenly than the compiler of this record.

On 28 February Monty Chalmers reported to the Directors that a fire had taken place the previous morning and had 'either totally destroyed or much injured' the *Journal* files. If, in the event, he was proved over-pessimistic, there was real tragedy in the fact that the earliest volumes suffered most. Some were destroyed altogether and the effect of that disastrous fire can still be seen on some of the surviving files. It seems, however, that some immediate consolation was provided by the insurance payment which enabled the Directors to order the painting of the premises.

A year later the firm was to suffer a further loss, this time through the death of one of its most outstanding Directors— P. H. Chalmers. He (with Colonel Innes of Learney) had been a leading figure in the founding of the first Aberdeen and North of Scotland Newspaper and Printing Company and had been its secretary during its lifetime and one of its most enthusiastic Directors during its second phase.

From the commercial front, however, more cheerful news was beginning to emerge. At the General Meeting of shareholders on 6 September 1889, the Chairman was able to report that, for the first time in its existence, the reconstituted Company could show a profit. The success was attributed to the fact that the *Journal* was recovering its old position as an advertising medium and to the increase in the sales of the *Evening Express*. At the same time the Directors felt it incumbent upon themselves to scold local Conservatives for failure to support the *Journal* as well as they should. It was not, by any means, the last time this admonition would be made.

We are apt to think of take-over bids as being a product of a later day and generation, but the history of the *Journal* is there to show that minds worked that way in the nineteenth, as well as the twentieth century. Was it mere coincidence that the turn in the fortunes of the Company should attract envious eyes in its direction? What do we find?

Soon Monty Chalmers was reporting that 'a gentleman representing the Gladstonian Party' had asked him whether there was any intention of selling the *Journal*. If so, the Gladstonian Party would be purchasers. Chalmers had rightly sensed the Directors' minds when he answered, 'No!'

Next to enter the arena was the *Free Press*, dangling £4,000 before the Directors, with just as little success as the Gladstonian Party had had. The *Journal* was not for sale and, to emphasise that fact, the Directors proceeded to put on record that they were highly satisfied with the progress of the Company. With the increase in circulation, advertisements and net profits, they considered that the stability and prospects were steadily improving. There was no intention to sell. And that was that!

Practical proof of this optimism was at once provided by the decision to buy a Hoe printing-machine which became the only one in Scotland capable of printing six-, eight- or twelve-page papers. And hereabouts comes a first hint that operations were becoming somewhat cramped in the existing premises, and the question rose whether to expand on the spot or to look around for new quarters. Things were to work out beyond the dreams of the Directors. But first, three matters concerning personnel.

The year 1890 saw Gillies back in the editorial chair. For some time the Directors had been anxious to secure his services again, and, although the first move proved discouraging, persistence brought its reward.

The same year saw the elevation of the Company's auditor, Augustus Sinclair, to the peerage—as the Earl of Caithness—and the consequent appointment of Walter A. Reid as auditor. It was the beginning of another long family link with the *Journal*.

But perhaps the year 1890 will be best remembered in the annals of the Company for the passing of John Gray Chalmers —on 31 October. He it was who, with his brother, sold the *Journal* to the private company, while continuing to play an active part in its progress. He it was who did so much for the University, the city and the Church. And now he was to dispel almost the last of the worries of the Directors of the Aberdeen and North of Scotland Newspaper and Printing Company with a munificent legacy of £10,000 to his trustees with instructions to devote the income to the promotion of the *Journal*'s interests. That it continues to do. Its terms have never been in dispute and the Sheriff, to whom such matters would have had to be referred by the terms of the legacy, has happily never had to give a ruling.

True, the time for paying dividends to the shareholders was some way off yet, but what was becoming more and more apparent was the unwavering plan and purpose of the Directors to build up the real, solid foundations of prosperity by seeing alike to improvement of plant and to the quality of their newspapers. Their eyes were less on profit than on consolidation. One cannot but admire the single-mindedness of those Directors who, in testing days, made no attempt at self-remuneration and worked consistently for the ultimate good of the firm.

Chapter 7

The story moves on to 1893, a red-letter year in the history of the Company, if ever there was one. It will be recalled that at the back of the minds of the Directors for some time had been considerations of office expansion. Indeed, some moves had been made to secure more elbow room, but these had not materialised and the problem did not become any less pressing.

How like manna from Heaven then must have come the report to the Acting Committee by Monty Chalmers that he had received a visit from the Secretary of the Northern Newspaper Company the purpose of which was to inquire whether the *Journal* firm would purchase their plant and premises in Broad Street. The Directors were quick to see that those premises could be admirably adapted to their needs, and, after a bit of haggling, the bargain was sealed at £5,625.

The *Northern News*, which the selling Company had published, was the first evening paper to be issued in Aberdeen. With its incorporation in the *Evening Express* the circulation of that paper jumped by 10,000. So, in its turn, the Aberdeen and North of Scotland Newspaper and Printing Company showed that it could make a pretty good take-over bid.

Considerable changes had, naturally, to be made in the Broad Street building—indeed alteration and addition became a continuous process down the years—and the Company was in no hurry to flit in its entirety. On 19 May 1894, however, came the celebrations to mark production in Broad Street.

But before then important editorial changes had been effected. Gillies had resigned as Editor on 28 February and had been succeeded by James McKay, from Cardiff, but hardly had he got into harness when he contracted a fatal illness. And so

David Pressly, an Aberdeen man working in Belfast, began his editorship practically with the flitting, a somewhat daunting prospect, but perhaps one relished by the redoubtable Pressly. He nailed his colours to the mast at a dinner to the staff, given as part of the celebrations.

'We mean,' he said, 'to go forward . . . I cannot say whether this new temple in Broad Street will ever equal the glory of the first, but I know that new opportunities will bring new responsibilities and new duties, and I am sure that every man on the staff, from first to last, means that it will not be through him that the ever-growing success of the *Journal* shall be abated.'

If the personal note may intrude again, there is a sense of continuity for the writer, then unborn, in the fact that present at that function were quite a number of men who were to be colleagues of his when he first passed, tremblingly, through the portals of Broad Street some 23 years later—names like those of J. A. C. Coutts, J. A. Nicol, J. Henderson, John Sleigh, A. Mitchell, A. Cumming, T. Crighton, W. Jaffrey, Peter Bird, David Jessiman, John Gall, Roddy M'Askill, J. Forbes, R. Wood, R. Fraser, J. Watt, W. Edwards, A. Cheyne, A. Gemmell, etc.

'We mean to go forward,' David Pressly had declared and it was in part fulfilment of that intention that a private wire to the firm's London office was introduced that very year. Robert Bruce, who was later to become Editor of the *Glasgow Herald* and to be knighted, was London Correspondent at the time. And so 5 New Bridge Street, London, became directly linked with the new premises in Broad Street to provide a more rapid and a greater flow of news and commentary from the metropolis. It was the beginning of many notable developments in this direction.

A contemporary description of the new home of the *Journal* indicates that, although the frontage was only 45 ft., there was an extensive range of buildings to the rear, 'carried to the boundary of the old prison in Lodge Walk, now to be converted into Police Buildings.' The venerable nature of the building, however, may be gathered from the fact that in one of its rooms, Isobel Pyper, wife of Baillie William Cruden, gave birth to a son on 31 May 1699, to whom they gave the name of Alexander. One of a family of eleven, he was educated at the Grammar School and at Marischal College where he graduated M.A. in 1721. He was to become universally known as the compiler of the famous *Complete Concordance of the Old and New Testaments*.

There is a story that links, somewhat unhappily, the names of Cruden and James Chalmers, founder of the *Journal*. Cruden had fallen desperately in love with a minister's daughter and, when the romance was rudely shattered, had broken down, mentally and physically. It was while he was on a visit to London, some years later, that Chalmers met the demented Cruden, and it was with the best intentions in the world that he suggested a visit to a house whose occupants he knew well. When the door opened, the wretched Cruden once more found himself face to face with the woman he had lost. Alas, the story has no happy ending. Cruden, it is recorded, turned away, his mind in a greater tumult than ever.

Back to Broad Street. In the new premises were three print-ing-machines—the Hoe, the Victory and the Simplex—proudly claimed by the Company to be the finest obtainable, capable, too, of meeting any emergency. The proprietors were, in fact, well prepared for the really prosperous years ahead, although caution was to be observed until it was absolutely certain that all was set fair. Not that good omens were not there. Share-holders at the 1895 meeting were to hear that profit had reached 'the handsome sum of practically £950, the largest ever made in one year,' that circulation was steadily improving as was revenue from other sources, notably advertising.

In the following year the profit nearly doubled itself and the question of introducing Linotype machines was discussed. Up to then all type had been set by hand. Eventually eight machines were bought—and they came none too soon for was it not said at this time that the sub-editors were handling daily as much copy as would have kept the *Journal* going, fifty years earlier, for about four months? One shies away from comparison with the situation today when news pours in ceaselessly, by human and mechanical means, to inundate the sub-editors' desks practically every hour of the day and night. Another straw in the wind was the fact that operative members of the staff were given a day's wages in lieu of a holiday on the occasion of the Queen's Diamond Jubilee (22 June 1897).

But the *Journal*'s 150th anniversary was a few months away and it was to mark that occasion that a facsimile copy of the first issue was produced, a reproduction in which Her Majesty expressed interest, in a letter sent by her Equerry to the Editor.

This, incidentally, is by no means the only occasion on which Royalty has paid tribute to a paper that is regularly read at Balmoral, although it is no longer necessary to take the special precautions which, Pressly's daughter recalled, her father saw in his day when the copy intended for Her Majesty was specially dried. The printer's art and his appliances have come a long way since then.

Milestone upon milestone, with name succeeding name in the hierarchy. On 6 October 1898, Esson asked to be relieved of the managership in order to engage in lighter duties and so James A. C. Coutts took over the commercial helm with his training as cashier to help him in his new sphere. His appointment dated from 1 January 1899. It was the beginning of a term of office that was to see the flowering of the patient efforts of the Directors to cultivate a delicate plant.

The previous year had seen the retirement, on pension, of one of the oldest servants of the Company, James Stewart. He had been continuously employed since 1846, and it is of interest to note that, through his son and grandsons, continuity was maintained. What changes these three generations have seen! They may be exemplified by the fact that one of the first directions of the new manager was to buy a typewriting machine and to engage a typist, the latter the first of a legion to brighten 'Broad Street'. What a blessing both would have been in the days of the illegible William Forsyth!

With the appointment, on 13 January, of Mr. William Ogg as Cashier the commercial regime assumed a shape familiar to many still alive. Mr. James A. Nicol was already there, on the advertising side, to complete the triumvirate.

One can recall the immaculate James Coutts moving through

the premises, humming 'The Old Hundred' and conjuring up we never knew what kind of a scheme; Willie Ogg, whose bark over reportorial expenses was ever worse than his bite; James Nicol, with his gold-encircled tie, cautious and difficult to better in any financial argument.

But though caution was still the watchword, there were wings to be stretched, new flights of fancy to be essayed. In March of that same year the manager was authorised to spend £20 to secure the exclusive right to advertise on the town tram tickets and to arrange with the Town Council for the right to sell the *Journal* on the streets.

Commercially the firm was on the move, but there were still handicaps to editorial progress. In April the Directors had before them a complaint about a *Journal* reporter 'calling late one evening at a house requesting information'. The opinion registered by the meeting was that more discretion ought to have been observed, and the Editor was requested to caution the staff generally against recurrence of visits of this nature. He was also asked to furnish the name of the reporter concerned.

One wonders what those Directors would have thought had they been able to peer down the years and see some of the strains and stresses of modern reporting.

Much seems to have happened in 1899. It's well nigh impossible to get away from it. We find, for instance, a David McCulloch, from Dingwall, being appointed to the staff 'in view of his certificate of competency as a reporter on agricultural matters'. It is a name that was to become well known in agricultural circles throughout the land. In the event his first stay with the firm proved a short one, but he was to return to the fold ere long and fit into the position for which he was so well qualified. Still in 1899, it was decided, for the time being, to defer issue of the Football Edition of the *Evening Express* and for the first time fees were paid to the Acting Committee of the Directors.

The autumn brought with it a new problem—that of delivering supplies to the city newsagents. Up to then the Tramway Company had undertaken that task, but they now announced

50

that the service was to be withdrawn. Confronted with this, the Directors decided to hire cycles for the time being and to ask estimates for the cost of building three carts, suited for horses of fifteen hands, 'the carts to be of a width not exceeding 5 ft. so that, if needs be, they might pass through Rettie's Court.'

The contract eventually went to Messrs. Webster Bros., Jopp's Lane, with the added instructions that the body was to be painted blue, the wheels red and the lettering white. The Company left no one in any doubt as to where their political allegiance lay.

And so we leave the nineteenth century with a flourish—a flourish that was to be taken up at once in the twentieth with the declaration of the Company's first dividend, albeit the modest one of $2\frac{1}{2}\%$.

Whether or not the Boer War was the main reason for the upsurge in the Company's fortunes it is difficult to say. At least it produced plenty of evidence of the live nature of journalism at the time, ever ready to try out new ideas. One example of this was the issue, by the *Evening Express*, of a contents bill, printed on linen, proclaiming the relief of Pretoria by Lord Roberts on 5 June 1900. It was topped by a line-drawing of Lord Roberts against a background of crossed Union Jacks, in full colour, and read:

EXPRESS
of Tuesday—contains
CAPTURE
OF
PRETORIA
OFFICIAL DESPATCH

This and other forms of enterprise undoubtedly helped sales, and even if the return to peace did affect these somewhat, there was more than compensation in the growth in advertising which, of itself, necessitated the printing of larger papers.

We hear a lot, these days, about the triumphs of colour printing, and Thomson Newspapers Ltd. have every reason to be proud of the success achieved by the *Sunday Times* Colour Supplement. But let it not be forgotten that, nigh on seventy years ago, the *Journal* was among the pioneers in this field, as it had been in so many other aspects of journalism.

In turn it had made special efforts to report fully and vividly the Coronations of George III, George IV, William IV and Queen Victoria, but all efforts in this direction were to be surpassed when Edward VII, following his operation for an abscess—not for the removal of his appendix, as was generally believed—was crowned on Saturday, 9 August 1902.

On the following Monday the *Journal* briefly announced: 'Today's issue, with its coloured cover in red, purple and chocolate, is the largest newspaper publication ever produced in Aberdeen.'

As far as the colour aspect is concerned, surely this was the under-statement of the year. Over and above the front page there were five pages in colour and, in addition to the shades mentioned, green and orange were utilised. True, the front page, with its etchings of the King and Queen, was the most impressive, but the others showed how much variation could be introduced, particularly in the reproduction of large advertisements.

The size of the paper itself was impressive at the time. It consisted of sixteen closely-printed, eight-column pages. Its very size seems to have created some misgivings in the minds of the publishers. At any rate, they saw fit to insert a notice inviting readers to make certain that they had got all sixteen pages!

The Royal Coronation Number, as it was sub-titled, made a tremendous impact upon the public and many bought several copies to send to friends and relatives overseas. It is a tribute to the foresight of the publishers that they had prepared special wrappers for this very purpose. They were in purple, the coronation colour, and on them were reproduced the Crown and Royal Arms.

The whole effort was perhaps best summed up by a correspondent who said it was a marvellous pennyworth. It represented, too, a tremendous triumph for the printers who tackled it, though what it cost them in 'blood and sweat and tears' they alone knew. Perhaps they, likewise, knew why their effort was not repeated in their day and generation. At any rate, strange stories of 'dismantling' have echoed down the years. Perhaps once in a lifetime was considered enough in those days, and it was not until 1963 that colour made its reappearance in the morning paper. Incidentally, those colour printing pioneers worked an 11-hour day and a six-day week.

Chapter 8

The year 1903 provided proof of further financial progress when it was decided to increase the dividend to 5%. It also brought a change in editorship, with Pressly leaving for Norwich and Robert Anderson moving over from the *Free Press* to succeed him.

With him Anderson brought a meticulous mind together with a broad outlook and a catholicity of interests. Born in London of Aberdeen parents (on 2 January 1848), he was educated at Robert Gordon's Hospital and he also attended classes at the University of Aberdeen. In 1862 he became a clerk in the Sheriff Clerk's office, holding for two years a commission as Sheriff Clerk Depute before answering the call of journalism. That was in 1873 when he joined the literary staff of the *Free Press*. Soon he was to become chief sub-editor and it was this post he held when the *Journal* appointment was offered to him.

As Editor, he was to prove a stickler for correct English and English without embellishment and without sensation. The latter was anathema to him; and a misplaced comma could bring forth sarcastic reprimand.

Apart from his newspaper work, he was perhaps best known for his editing of the fourth edition of Dr. Pratt's *Buchan*, published in 1901. He was also author of a historical volume on Robert Gordon's Hospital, of *Aberdeen In Byegone Days* and *Walks Round Aberdeen*. As to the diversity of his interests, perhaps that is best conveyed by his club memberships which included the University Club, the New Spalding Club, the Aberdeen Philosophical Society, the Buchan Field Club, the Cairngorm Club and Gordon's Hospital Old Boy's Association.

Other days, other ideas. How different now is the conception of what constitutes a broad street. At any rate, in their lay-out of Broad Street the planners of yesterday set their successors no small problem. True, the opening of King Street helped considerably, but that was but a temporary solution, even though it silenced the critics for a century.

In 1904 came the hint that civic minds were being directed to the possibility of doing something about it. The idea that found favour involved a new alignment of the *Journal* buildings, for the records of the firm show that 'a reasonable sum of compensation' was worked out. But that was as far as the scheme got. It was shelved, as have been others of similar good intention, more of which anon. It was not until sixty years after this first tentative move that purpose began to assume actual shape. The plans had been changed somewhat. Buildings on the other—the west—side of Broad Street were demolished and the widening process was thus designed to accommodate the long-discussed plan for new Municipal Buildings.

Now, as the French would say, let's return to our sheep. We left the *Journal* on a happy financial note. It was one that was to sound louder and louder as the years rolled by. At the 21st anniversary General Meeting the Chairman was able to make a striking comparison. In 1884, he said, the liabilities of the Company were £23,342 compared with £29,950 and assets £19,742 against £33,598. There was a loss of £1,266 against a profit of £3,418. These figures tell their own story. The Company had come a long way since those threatening days of the 'eighties. The dividend—now 7½%—spoke volumes as well.

Personalities have meant much in the success of the firm, both on the editorial and the commercial side. Names keep cropping up for the first time in the records. Like that of George Sleigh, engaged in 1907 and promoted four years later to take charge of the sporting news and to become widely known for many years under the pseudonym of 'Spec'.

Hereabouts came the first realisation of the growing needs of transport for reportorial purposes. All things need a beginning. In 1908 it was decided to engage a motor car to enable reporters to cover twenty meetings planned by Colonel Burn in an attempt to win East Aberdeenshire. Was it a sign of the times and the attitude towards such expense that the chief reporter saw to it that the car was required on only one occasion? Or is it that chief reporters are just built that way?

With success still the watchword, even when depression hit other industries, the Directors had a mind to further house expansion. It was with this in view that they made inquiries regarding the adjoining premises, occupied by Messrs. Mc-Killiam, bakers, but the negotiations fell through, and that section of the building was not to become part of the firm's property, at any rate for the time being. Night sub-editors of those days used to be regaled with somewhat bucolic strains from the numerous wedding parties and other functions held in the small hall attached to the bakery which was later to become the home of the telegraphic news and picture receiving and transmitting apparatus of Aberdeen Journals Ltd.

The year 1910 brought another change at the editorial helm, William Maxwell, from the London *Evening Standard*, taking over from Robert Anderson who had retired. A Kirkcudbright man, Maxwell was educated at a private school where S. R. Crockett, the novelist, was a junior master. It was the beginning of a lifelong friendship. An alumnus of Glasgow University, Maxwell received a comprehensive training in the commercial, mechanical and editorial aspects of newspaper work, under the guidance of his father, owner of the leading county paper in the Stewartry.

For a while he worked in Hull and York before returning to Scotland to join the staff of the *Scotsman*. Crossing the Border again, he was, for a year, in the late 'nineties, Managing Editor of a group of papers at Taunton, before moving to London where, in a twelve-year period, he was, successively, news editor of the *St. James's Gazette*, news editor of the *Pall Mall Gazette* and chief sub-editor and night news editor of the *Evening Standard* with Edgar Wallace, of thriller fame, as one of his colleagues.

The new Editor speedily adapted himself to the north-east environment. He ran slap-bang into the Dee–Avon water dispute, and it was largely due to his advocacy that the Dee party won the day. This was no mere fluoride affair. The battle for the source of Aberdeen's water supply assumed far greater proportions than that 'stramash'. The *Free Press* had plumped for the Avon and it was a typical Maxwell flourish to proclaim his paper's victory by means of a contents bill on which was printed a huge letter D—and nothing else.

A staunch and fighting Tory, Maxwell at once applied himself to what seemed then the hopeless task of converting northeast allegiance from Liberalism to Unionism, and perhaps he considered it his greatest triumph, as the seemingly impossible was achieved in overwhelming measure.

One of his first moves—and events were to prove how farsighted it was—was to recommend to the Directors the appointment of William Veitch as literary head of the London Office. And so began, on 1 October 1910, an association with the *Journal* (later *The Press and Journal*) ended only by his death on 12 August 1975. It was, indeed, thanks to correspondence between Maxwell and Veitch that the writer was able to read the editorial mind of the day and to appreciate the ambitions of the new Editor.

First of these was to bring the circulation of the *Journal* more into line with that of the *Evening Express*. Later Maxwell was to claim that, in ten years' time, that ambition had been realised.

Secondly, he had it in mind to make the morning paper pre-eminent over the *Scotsman* and the *Glasgow Herald* as the national Scottish newspaper; and it was to this end that he arranged for a greater coverage of national news so as to rescue the *Journal* from being the 'mere local newspaper' he considered it to be at the time.

With economy, however, still the watchword, it was essential to find savings somewhere to meet the new bills and the correspondence provides many sidelights on the scrutiny of reportorial expenses and on the tight rein that had to be kept on salaries. There were complaints, too, concerning the cost of covering the Smithfield Show, the Stock Exchange and Parliamentary proceedings, all showing that the desired progress had to be tackled on a very restricted budget. It is little wonder that there were times when Veitch felt that the London end was being saddled with all the economies.

A big change during the early days of the Maxwell regime was the introduction of the Creed-Bille wiring system between Aberdeen and the London office at 5 New Bridge Street. Before then the Aberdeen–London private wire was operated by Post Office telegraphists, using the old Morse key system. It was one of the handicaps that these operators removed, each morning, the wired 'copy' as this was regarded as Post Office property. It can be appreciated how awkward this could be when reference to such 'copy' was subsequently necessary. Whether or not that was possible depended, it seems, on the goodwill or otherwise of the telegraphist concerned. With the Creed installation the *Journal* employed its own staff, and this solved that particular problem, at the same time introduced a method of transmission vastly improved in volume, speed, readability and accuracy.

With Messrs. McKilliam still holding out, the possibility of securing elbow room at the other end of the Broad Street frontage arose when the owner and occupant of No. 24, a Mr. Fleming, expressed readiness to do a deal. As the Directors, like Barkis, were willing, it went through. The premises were to be let to Fleming until such time as the Company required them.

On 16 September 1911, the Football Edition of the *Evening Express* made its reappearance, to strong competition from the *Gazette*. It was but one of a succession of moves designed to provide a news service in accordance with the Company's aims. And it had to be up-to-the-minute news, as an order, that same autumn, to purchase Late News Devices (a Stop Press system) would readily suggest.

Staff changes on 1 January 1912, should be recorded. First, Alexander Catto, who had been chief sub-editor of the *Evening Express*, was appointed chief reporter, a post which made him one of the best known journalists in the north-east. To succeed him on the *Express* staff J. R. Pettigrew was induced to come from Glasgow and Douglas Maxwell, son of the Editor, became his assistant. Less than eighteen months later tragedy was to strike grimly at both and, through them, at the *Evening Express*. On 25 May 1913, both were killed as the result of a motoring accident.

Meanwhile all was going well on the commercial front. The circulation of the *Evening Express* had risen to 45,500 and all seemed set fair for further progress. The clouds of war had not yet loomed up, but they were gathering beyond the horizon and when the flood-gates were opened on 4 August 1914, a very different situation confronted the newspaper world.

First and foremost came the problem of staff. Like so many other young men of the day, the youthful—and some not so youthful—members were among the earliest volunteers. Before it was all over the equivalent of half the number of the pre-war employees had gone to the wars. But that was only one aspect of the problem. Rising costs of news services, of newsprint, of ink and wages combined with falling revenue from advertisements and other sources. To offset these, however, was the rise in circulation, with readers avid to study the diminishing columns, often, alas, the bearers of tragic tidings as the battles took their grim toll and names like Loos, Neuve Chapelle, the Somme, Passchendaele became symbols alike of heroism and sacrifice.

By 1916 the average sales of the *Express* had mounted to 56,700.

Co-operation manifested itself in many ways during World War I. It produced, for instance, a readiness between the Directors of the *Journal* and the proprietors of the *Free Press* to conclude working agreements—on restriction of paper sizes, on mutual reportorial aid, on advertising charges and on the abolition of contents bills and returns of unsold copies by newsagents. It was the hour that dictated these arrangements and, when the circumstances that suggested them no longer prevailed, it is probably right to say that their lesson was not entirely forgotten. Perhaps they were the outriders of an amalgamation of forces yet to come, though still a good five years away.

Price increases became inevitable. First it was the *Express* that went up from a halfpenny to a penny, to be followed, shortly afterwards, by a halfpenny rise in the *Journal* to three halfpence, the opposition, of course, doing likewise.

Again the personal note: it does keep obtruding. On 26 September 1917, it seems, the Editor informed the Directors of the need for an additional sub-editor for the *Journal* and found them in an acquiescent mood, with the proviso that the new man would be paid at the rate of '25/– a week for six months and 30/– thereafter'. It was not a princely sum to offer a graduate. Perhaps the strange additional bait Maxwell held out suggested a recognition of that fact. Journalism, he said, was a healthy occupation. Most journalists lived to a ripe old age, a less attractive proposition, be it said, to the young man than it was when the time came for him to retire. Incidentally, the man of promise lived himself to the age of eighty-five. At least he did his personal best to prove his point!

Anyway, the young man fell for the bait—and things did not turn out too badly for him in the long run. In his introduction to journalism Alexander Keith, a fellow graduate, had been the intermediary. He had joined the staff some nine months earlier and was soon to become leader-writer and assistant editor of the *Journal*. Eventually he was to become the well-known secretary of the Aberdeen-Angus Society, with a term as President of the Aberdeen Chamber of Commerce, and a progressive farmer with the bent for writing not entirely suppressed. In 1967 his Alma Mater was to honour him by conferring on him an LL.D. degree.

Peace restored, the old commercial rivalries naturally took shape again, but that did not prevent the *Journal* from having a fellow feeling for the *Free Press* when a disastrous fire played havoc with its means of production. That was on 23 July 1919. There came a ready response from the *Journal* Directors, and the aid then provided was continued until such time as the proprietors of the *Free Press* were able to replace the destroyed machinery and stand on their own feet again. This readiness to help a rival in distress is a well-established tradition in the newspaper industry.

True, a little bit of journalistic devilment did creep in when a *Journal* upmaker inserted a bold 'house ad.', proclaiming the superior virtues of *Journal* agricultural reports, in a page prepared for publication in the *Free Press*. If the *Free Press* proprietors were 'not amused', at least the late Sir William Maxwell was. His chuckle assured the 'comp.', not long back from the wars, that he had not jeopardised his future. In point of fact, he ultimately went over to the editorial side and in due course became assistant to the Editor of *The Press and Journal*.

But whatever opinions may have been at the time, they did not interfere in any way with discussions of a more vital nature which began a little over a year later—discussions on no less a matter than the possible amalgamation of the two firms. Maxwell's commentary on these proposals was typical of the man. His correspondence with Veitch reveals that they were initiated by John Bruce, one of the *Free Press* proprietors, through a third party.

'On our part,' wrote Maxwell, 'we would have bought them up, but their own idea of the value of their property was absurd and there were other stipulations regarding the title, etc., which our Directors could not entertain, although the conversations had not broken off completely when Bruce died.'

Subsequent events showed that it takes two to make a bargain. In any case a compromise was reached and it was possible to present to an Extraordinary Meeting of the *Journal* shareholders, on 3 November 1922, an Agreement for Amalgamation.

This provided, among other things, for the liquidation of the Aberdeen and North of Scotland Newspaper and Printing Company Limited and for the sale of its assets to a new Company to be called Aberdeen Newspapers Limited. Similarly the *Free Press* assets were to be assigned to the new Company.

The marriage was to be symbolised by the name of the combined morning paper which was now to be called *The Aberdeen Press and Journal*. In the event the name of the *Gazette* disappeared altogether and the continuity of the *Evening Express* was thus maintained.

As for the Directorate, this was to consist of the existing members of the *Journal* Board with the addition of the four partners of the *Free Press*—Messrs. Henry Alexander, William

McCombie Alexander, Robert Bruce, whose father had set things on foot, and Edward William Watt, the latter three to receive, in addition, paid appointments.

The Instrument of Agreement, which was passed, was dated 20 October 1922.

At this point it is essential once more to turn the clock back in order to summarise the history of the *Free Press* which had now become an integral part of *The Aberdeen Press and Journal*. It had been founded as *The Aberdeen Free Press and North of Scotland Review: a General Advertiser for Aberdeen and the Northern Counties* on 6 May 1853 as successor to the *North of Scotland Gazette* which had had a run of only six years. In that short time it had introduced to the public William Carnie, one of Aberdeen's most distinguished journalists, the benefit of whose ability and experience was at once secured by William M'Combie, David Macallan and George King, the founders of the *Free Press*.

With the abolition of the Stamp Duty, the proprietors thought they saw an opportunity for development. Their ideas took the shape of a cheaper Tuesday issue over and above the usual Friday one. But it would seem that the public were not yet ready for such an experiment and the *Penny Free Press*, as it was called, was dropped after a run of only eight months.

But those *Free Press* founders were determined men, and a revitalised Tuesday issue was tested out again in 1865, this time with success, so much so that, seven years later, the proprietors were emboldened to introduce a daily issue, the first experience of its kind for Aberdeen and the north-east. They had beaten the *Journal* for this honour by four years.

Through all the ups and downs that followed, the *Aberdeen Daily Free Press* strove hard to maintain the high traditions set by William M'Combie, its first Editor, who had made a reputation as an essayist as well as a journalist. And there is no need to remind those who know their 'Johnny Gibb of Gushetneuk' of the place M'Combie's successor, Dr. William Alexander, had in the hearts of the men and women of the north-east, wherever they were to be found the world over.

Throughout its individual history the *Free Press* remained

loyal to the Liberal cause, a loyalty for which, there is no doubt, it paid dearly during the slump in the north, as elsewhere throughout Britain, in that party's appeal, in the face of the rising tide of Socialism and the growing strength of Conservatism in the area.

In the end the wiser course became abundantly clear.

It is but natural that everything else that happened to the *Journal* in 1922 should be overshadowed by the amalgamation with the *Free Press*, but there was one fling the older partner had which must not pass unnoticed. In its way it set up a new standard in newspaper enterprise and, indeed, in aviation.

At the time the only regular transport service between London and Aberdeen was that afforded by the railway, and this meant that pictures of the Derby finish normally reached Aberdeen far too late for reproduction in the *Journal*.

It was to get round this—and, incidentally, to steal a march on the opposition—that an arrangement was made with the Picture House (now the Gaumont) proprietors to fly from London a film for the cinema and photo prints for the *Journal*; and, to ensure the success of the project, the one and only Sir Alan Cobham was engaged to pilot the plane.

The date was 31 May 1922, and the winner Captain Cuttle. As for the flight north, the measure of the enterprise can best be judged by the fact that it proved to be the fastest long, non-stop flight in the British Isles up to then. But, still further to expedite matters, it was arranged for Sir Alan to drop the film and prints by parachute, with Torry Hill as the target.

In the event, the parachute became entangled in the rudder wires and before it had worked clear the plane was over Torry itself and the parachute actually landed in the backyard of the tenement at 161 Victoria Road where it was picked up by a youngster, Alexander Russell, who, sensing the significance of the attached packet, ran with it, accompanied by a chum, all the way to the Picture House. The film was forthwith screened and the pictures were hurried to the *Journal* Process Department where plates were produced in time to catch all editions.

The pictures published were a side-on view of Captain Cuttle winning by four lengths from Tamar, with Craiganour third, a head-on one of the finish and the parade scene before the start.

Meanwhile Sir Alan had flown on to the Black Dog, guided by a bonfire promptly lit by the man in charge when he heard the sound of the approaching plane. Incidentally it was the first time Sir Alan had ever seen Aberdeen!

Chapter 9

To amalgamate in name is one thing: to forge a new, effective instrument from a plethora of parts, human and mechanical, is quite another matter, and many decisions had to be taken before the composite machine could settle down to the smooth working essential in newspaper production.

First there had to be choice of buildings. In the event it was decided to operate from Broad Street. In this conclusion Maxwell had more than a little say. He it was who insisted upon the retention of the old *Journal* office even though the *Free Press* building was the better one. It was not in his nature to permit any indication other than that the *Journal* was 'taking over' the *Free Press*. It is just possible that, as a sort of counterpoise, the *Free Press* London office at 149 Fleet Street was preferred to the *Journal* one in New Bridge Street.

Staffing naturally presented a major problem, apart from the editorship which was assigned to William Maxwell as part of the Agreement. On a similar basis James Coutts and Edward Watt became joint managers, William Alexander editor of the subsidiary productions and Robert Bruce London manager. With staffs duplicated in every department a judicious selection had to be made and where it was found impossible to provide employment compensation was paid.

Gradually the new team settled in. New faces became 'kent' faces and community of purpose welded the parts into an effective whole. Meanwhile the sense of continuity had been further assured by the retention of the *Journal* and *Express* serial numbering.

With the turn of the year the old question of the widening of Broad Street cropped up again and we find the Directors discussing a plan which, had it materialised, would have involved the purchase by the Town Council of the Broad Street buildings and the construction by the firm of entirely new premises on a site in Exchequer Row, the property of the Town and now the site for a multi-storeyed car park and self-service store.

Negotiations with the Lord Provost, the City Treasurer and the City Chamberlain followed and, for a time, it seemed that the deal would go through, particularly as the Town House was already incapable of housing the growing departments and new quarters had to be found somewhere. In the end, however, nothing came of it. For the Town it was stated that the widening of Broad Street was not contemplated for many years to come, nor was the enlargement of the Town House in view of the fact that the additional accommodation required had been found elsewhere. In the light of what happened in the long run it would seem that the City Fathers were not as far-sighted as they might have been.

It might be added here that, in the late 'thirties, the erection of new *Press and Journal* buildings was envisaged at the corner of Upper Kirkgate and Broad Street. Architects drew up plans in detail and deep drillings were made to discover whether a subterranean stream would interfere with the foundations of any new building. Negotiations were opened up with the City Treasurer. Five minutes later they were closed, abruptly and finally.

With the Broad Street deal off, the Directors did not immediately abandon the idea of building in Exchequer Row, but in the end what were considered excessive demands by the Town's representatives put a damper on the whole business and it came to nothing. In any case it had, at last, been possible to acquire the desired next-door McKilliam premises as well as other buildings, in Chronicle Court, and expansion on the spot became a more practical prospect. As the Directors visualised it, 'alterations would enable the Company to carry on in Broad Street until such times as further purchase towards Queen Street could be made when a comprehensive scheme of reconstruction for the subjects, as they might then be, could be

66

arranged.' And if that wasn't far-sightedness, what is? All the purchases envisaged were ultimately made, much in the way of reconstruction was carried out—until such time as a much more ambitious scheme emerged. But more of that anon.

The immediate future, as far as premises were concerned, having been settled, the Company decided to sell the *Free Press* building in Union Street and Messrs. Esslemont and Macintosh seized the opportunity to add that very fine building to their property. It is perhaps of interest to note that around coffee-time a number of Broad Street journalists began to frequent the firm's restaurant where once men of the same calling tackled the sterner tasks of newspaper production.

Plant improvements continue to be recorded, including the installation of an electricity generator because of breakdowns in the public supply, particularly during the night. That was in 1924.

The following year brought the decision to shift the London Office from 149 Fleet Street to 130 Fleet Street. It also saw the appointment of William Maxwell as a Director and brought the Directors' congratulations to Henry Alexander on his election to the Town Council. And so the year seemed to be moving quietly and happily to its close.

Then, like a bolt from the blue, came a crisis in the Company's affairs. There have always been two sides to the story as to what actually happened.

From the time of the amalgamation, it would seem, the *Free Press* section of the Directorate had been dissatisfied with Maxwell's interpretation of 'Constitutionalism' which was the policy agreed to in the course of the negotiations, and for them it can be said that there had been little departure from the old Conservative and Imperial point of view which the *Journal* had for long championed. At any rate, the gravamen of the charge against the *Free Press* Directors was that they had attempted to sell their shares to a prominent Liberal and so pave the way to ultimate Liberal control of the firm. This was denied and it was claimed that any share deal envisaged was a normal transaction with no ulterior motive.

In the end three of the four *Free Press* Directors resigned

67

office. The one exception was Robert Bruce who had had nothing whatsoever to do with the bit of bother no matter what its nature. He retained his directorship, but he gave up his appointment as London manager, a post to which William J. Peters succeeded. Subsequently Henry Alexander and Edward Watt were to devote their talents to civic work, each in turn to become Lord Provost of the city.

Meanwhile, in Broad Street, James Coutts assumed anew all the duties of managership and the ruffled waters became calm again, if ever that can be said of a newspaper office. In point of fact another storm was brewing, of a very different order and with nation-wide implications. It was only months away.

Hitherto, in the history of the Company, labour relations had been maintained on a healthy plane. There had been disputes over wages and conditions, but these had been of a minor order and were practically always settled on an amicable basis and actual production of the Company's newspapers had never been in real danger. Some of the troubles, in fact, had something of a comical aspect. The late Tom Crighton, a venerable compositor, used to tell such a tale of his apprenticeship days. He and one or two other apprentices, dissatisfied with a financial arrangement over the correction of the type they used to set up, decided to lay their case before the formidable head printer, Mr. Jolly. Jolly, with his ear always close to the ground, obviously had a pretty good idea of what was in the wind as he saw the deputation drawing towards him. At any rate, the look he gave its members as he drew himself up to his full height was too much for them. As Tom would say, when recalling the experience, 'we thought better of it and fled without a word having been spoken on either side.'

It was a very different state of affairs, however, when all efforts to end the mining dispute failed and the General Strike was called for 4 May 1926. The country's newspapers, in common with all other commercial and industrial concerns, at once found themselves up against it.

With the order to strike not coming into operation until the end of the night-shift, it was found possible to publish the morning paper as usual on 4 May, but for the next five days the best that could be done was to issue Strike Editions, consisting of a single typewritten sheet. These were sold at a penny.

Looked at from a purely journalistic point of view, these issues were remarkable efforts in news condensing. They covered the national and the local aspects of the strike, described available transport facilities, reported Parliamentary debates, including the historic pronouncement of Sir John Simon about the illegality of the strike which ultimately brought about its collapse, provided the latest Stock Exchange quotations and indicated, generally, commodity market and sporting activities, with particular reference to racing and cricket. But it was never claimed for them that they were other than a stopgap. The serial numbering, in fact, was not applied to them. That was not picked up again until 11 May when normal methods of publication, though on a reduced scale, were resumed. The point is made lest someone with a bent for these things should, one day, stumble upon a seeming hiatus.

Meanwhile the Directors were keeping close watch on the situation. One safeguard they decided upon was to 'insure against damage by riot and civil disobedience to the buildings and their contents.' Happily, no claim fell to be met.

Much more important was the decision to make the Company a non-union one and to publish a notice to this effect. This invited applications from former members of the staff for reinstatement on this basis. At the same time they were guaranteed payment by the firm of benefits of not less value than those provided by the unions. The vast majority of the employees accepted these terms. By 13 May, in any case, the General Strike had collapsed, and gradually the size of the papers was stepped up to normal dimensions. It had been an unhappy experience for employers and employees alike, though relieved to some extent by the lack of recrimination when it was all over. The real tragedy lay in the fact that no dispute existed at the time between the firm and its staff. It was, in short, a strike that ought never to have been.

It was not, however, without its lighter side, as two instances may serve to illustrate. Maxwell had made a point of interviewing, individually, members of the editorial staff who wanted reinstatement. To eacn ne delivered something in the nature of a homily and most crept from the editorial sanctum somewhat chastened—in appearance, at least. But Maxwell, for all his moments of fire and fury, was generally quick to recover his good nature and when John Ogilvie, whose dry humour was proverbial in the office, appeared 'on the carpet' the homily was dispensed with.

'Why on earth,' asked Maxwell, 'did a sensible person like you, John, go on strike?'

'Well, Mr Maxwell,' replied the quick-witted John, 'I had never been on strike before and I wanted to study one from within.'

Maxwell's anger—or what was left of it—dissolved in hearty laughter. 'Away you go, John!' he chortled. 'I might have known that you would have a wonderful get-out.'

It must have been in this mood that Maxwell confronted a very young Peter Craighead (later to become news editor). 'You don't look like a revolutionary,' he said. 'Get back to your work!' And Peter, one can be pretty sure, stayed not upon the order of his going.

On from fateful 1926 to 1927 which was to bring changes of a different order, this time in the editorial set-up, fore-shadowed by a report, on 22 April, to the Directors that William Maxwell, the Editor, was ill. He had become a victim to phlebitis. It soon became apparent that immediate recovery was not to be expected, and he resigned on 30 August. He had held the editorial chair for seventeen years, years of remark-able financial progress by the Company for which, the Directors recorded, he was largely responsible.

Happily, Maxwell made a good recovery and was able to maintain his journalistic link via the boardroom. To this activity he added a renewed interest in politics, identifying himself with the workings of the South Aberdeen Unionist Association, and it was for his services to both that a knight-hood was conferred upon him in the 1928 New Year Honours. A further honour came his way the following year when he was appointed President of the South Aberdeen Unionist Association and there was a period when he was Convener or

President of no fewer than four Unionist organisations. Sir William, as has already been indicated, lived to the age of eighty-five. He died at his home in Bon-Accord Square, Aberdeen, on 20 May 1947. His great journalistic idol, he once told the writer, was John T. Delane, the famous Editor of *The Times*. In many ways he modelled himself on that pillar of the 'Thunderer'.

When the post was advertised, many sought the editorship of the Aberdeen newspapers, a tribute itself to their high standing, and in the end the decision of the Directors was to appoint the London Editor, William Veitch, Editor-in-Chief of the morning and weekly papers with consultative control over the evening paper which, for production purposes, was to come under the editorial control of Alexander Catto, then chief reporter. It was an arrangement that worked less well in practice than theory had suggested, and the matter was finally resolved when Catto was appointed news editor and Veitch retained the full editorship of all the Company's publications.

Educated at George Watson's College, Veitch had entered journalism via the Edinburgh *Evening Dispatch*, and his long association with the Aberdeen papers began in 1910 when he was appointed London Editor, a position in which he made a name for himself in Fleet Street and in the Parliamentary Press Gallery of which he became Chairman. He was also General Treasurer of the National Union of Journalists and played a leading part in that body's deliberations.

It was with this reputation that he came to fill the editorial chair in Aberdeen, to begin, as it proved, an editorship that was to see not only great advances and great changes but to extend, in years, far beyond the tenure of that office by any of his predecessors since the Chalmers' days.

Chapter 10

If 1926 and 1927 brought their excitements in the affairs of the Company, something of a much bigger order was being reserved for 1928. It was on 2 March of that year that the Directors got the first hint of Lord Rothermere's plan to inaugurate a chain of *Evening Worlds*, as he was to call them, up and down the country and to include Aberdeen in the set-up. Things developed rapidly and, by the following month, the Directors had before them rival offers from Allied Newspapers Limited and Northcliffe Newspapers Limited for the purchase of the Company.

A price battle ensued and lasted well into the autumn, with the main body of the Directors favouring the Allied Newspapers offer, even if it did seem less attractive on purely financial grounds. In the end their view prevailed, and on 31 October, at an Extraordinary General Meeting, a motion was carried for the liquidation of Aberdeen Newspapers Limited, with James A. C. Coutts as liquidator. The process was completed on 16 November. But, though Aberdeen Newspapers Limited sank into its grave, from the ashes arose forthwith a new Company, not so very different in name. It was as Aberdeen Journals Limited that the old firm became part of the great Allied Newspapers group.

The history of the formation of this group would take a volume in itself, but here we must be content with a brief look at the two men who had been responsible for its creation and development.

The progress of the Berry Brothers (as they were then known)—William Ewart Berry (later Viscount Camrose) and James Gomer Berry (later Viscount Kemsley)—is one of the great romances of the newspaper world.

72

Starting with a capital of less than £100, the Berry Brothers built up a newspaper empire which was to spread its influence all over Britain. It was the combination of their qualities—business acumen, flair for news, literary skill and vision, combined with a readiness to take risks—that enabled them to make such remarkable progress; and, if we care to look ahead a bit at this stage, it will be to discover that, when they decided in 1937 to go their separate ways, each was to continue to pursue success and achieve it in overwhelming measure.

To be in the Allied Newspapers group was, of course, to be in one of the biggest newspaper chains in the world. The advantages soon became apparent. With an organisation of this nature behind them the Aberdeen newspapers were able to give a much more comprehensive news service to their readers. A far-flung foreign service, organised by Ian Fleming of thriller fame and supplied by the group's own correspondents, became available, and this was backed up with a fuller coverage of home news, with particular reference to the requirements of the north-east, the north and the islands in the circulation area. Better feature articles became available and new ideas in journalism were promoted at regular group conferences. At the same time steps were taken to inaugurate a training scheme for journalists.

But it was not only in this latter respect that journalists benefited. Opportunity, both positional and financial, presented itself and status got a decided fillip. Before long, too, employees were to be provided with an opportunity to rejoin their trades unions, if they so wished, while the rights of those who wished to retain the status quo were safeguarded. The new employers, in fact, preferred to negotiate through the unions. Events showed that most of the employees were of the same frame of mind.

July 31, 1929, is yet another day for the Company's records, and for two reasons. On that day David Montagu Alexander Chalmers, of Messrs. C. & P. H. Chalmers, who had for so long carried out the firm's secretarial duties, died; and so the last direct link with the *Journal*'s founder, as far as the

Aberdeen newspapers are concerned was snapped. A bachelor and in manner and bearing a relic of the Victorians, he had worked with tremendous enthusiasm for the firm and in that respect, as in others, he was true to ancestral type.

On that day, too, James A. C. Coutts, who had upheld the burden of management for thirty years and had given forty-five years of service, relinquished the commercial helm while agreeing to carry on as advising Director. He had steered the Northern Newspaper and Printing Company through its most difficult years and had built prosperity upon prosperity. He had played a leading role in the amalgamation of Aberdeen's newspapers and was similarly engaged in the battle royal between Allied Newspapers and Northcliffe Newspapers for their control.

The occasion of his retirement was not allowed to pass without due recognition. At a public dinner he was presented with his portrait in oils, the work of John A. M. Hay, the Aberdeen artist.

On that occasion he recalled how, when he was appointed manager, he copied an article which set down a series of hints as to what he should do. Perhaps the one that most neatly fits his own approach is that which admonished him to 'bear in mind that, eventually, there must be a satisfactory ratio between expenses and income.' He, it can be said without hesitation, achieved that—and perhaps a bit more: nay, much more.

The staff did not forget him. The occasion found him in reminiscent and humorous vein. He recalled, in his pawky way, how he once went to New Aberdour to initiate a new agent—a shoemaker named Gerrard—into the mysteries of advertising rates and was pleased to note that the *Journal* contents bill occupied nearly all the show-window space. But when he congratulated the 'soutar' on this he was to be met with that worthy's counter: 'Oh, aye, the bill comes in handy for keepin' the sun fae the beets.' And nobody would have appreciated more than James Coutts that shaft of Buchan wit.

At that same function he remarked that the action of the staff had so rejuvenated him that he felt he stood a sporting

74

chance of participating in the celebration of the 200th anniversary of the founding of the *Journal* in 1948—well, he did not quite make it. He died on 15 April 1941. Something of a legend passed with him, certainly for those who knew him and worked in his company.

It is perhaps of interest to note that, on the same day, the remains of Dr. Charles Murray, better known as 'Hamewith' (though he never liked that designation), were cremated in Aberdeen. The *Journal*, incidentally, had been privileged to give first publication to two of his finest descriptive poems: 'Dockens Before His Peers' and 'There's Aye A Something'. No doubt his friend Alex Keith exercised his considerable persuasive powers to this end.

The point may be made here, too, that 'Broad Street' had been the springboard as well for two of the best northern novelists of the century: James Leslie Mitchell (Lewis Grassic Gibbon) and Eric Linklater, the former as a 'cub' reporter, the latter seeking journalistic experience before setting out for India.

James Coutts had outlived one of the triumvirate. William Ogg, for so long the firm's cashier, had died ten years earlier—on 5 January 1931, to be exact—but the third member, James A. Nicol, advertising manager for an even longer period, survived until 9 April 1946. Ogg, like Coutts, had arrived in the newspaper world via the banking profession, and it might be noted that all three were of country stock. Nicol, like Coutts, hailed from the Echt district and had vivid recollections of the famous Dunecht mystery. He used to recall how, as a lad, he helped Scotland Yard detectives, aided by bloodhounds, in their search for the missing body of the Earl of Crawford and Balcarres.

But here we must retrace our steps somewhat, back to that eventful year of 1929, to record, that on 20 January the *Evening Express* attained its jubilee. It was an occasion for looking back and, as must ever be the case with progressive newspapers, forward.

The *Evening Express* had come a long way since its first, tentative introduction to the public. It had consolidated its hold, particularly on the city of Aberdeen, and was steadily extending its influence all over the north-east. It had become a valuable advertising medium and had had not a little to do with the solid financial progress of the Company. It had championed many worthy causes and had acted as the watchdog on all that pertained to the well-being of the north-east. It had been both a spur and a corrective—a worthy scion in every way of its progenitor, the old, but ever young, morning paper.

Chapter 11

Reference has been made to some of the advantages of becoming part of the Allied Newspapers combination. Perhaps the greatest one of all derived from the group's identification with the interests of the area served by the Aberdeen newspapers. To gain local knowledge and experience in newspaper production members of both branches of the family, in turn, shared in the work of producing the Aberdeen papers. Most fruitful of all these associations was that created by the Hon. Pamela Berry, daughter of Lord Kemsley, who was to find romance in our midst and play a leading part in the social life of the north-east as the Marchioness of Huntly, wife of the premier Marquess of Scotland.

Identification with the north-east's interests took many other forms, not the least of them those of a charitable character and those directed towards the furthering of education. For many years, under the earlier regimes, it had been customary for both the morning and the evening paper to raise funds for the alleviation of distress or to help with some worthy project. Publicity, for instance, helped to swell the sum raised on behalf of the victims of the Dee Ferry Boat Disaster on 5 April 1876, when thirty-two lives were needlessly lost.

In 1886 over £1,000 was subscribed by readers of the *Evening Express* towards the relief of the unemployed. Ten years later £1,081 was raised by both papers following a succession of sea disasters.

On the outbreak of the Boer War a fund was opened to assist 'Those Left Behind'—the widows and children of those who fell and the children of Reservists ordered to the front. Within a year £4,619 had been subscribed, the largest amount raised by public subscription, by any newspaper north of Edinburgh and Glasgow.

The gale disasters round our coast in 1912 again brought ready response to the newspapers' appeal. On 14 January the Dundee steamer *Clio* was driven ashore at Cairnbulg Point. At Spey Bay, two days later, the Buckie fishing boat *Sublime* was wrecked and several of the crew perished. On the 17th the *Frederick Snowden* (from Shields to Aberdeen with coal) turned turtle off Port Errol, with the loss of all hands. On the 18th the *Wistow Hall* was wrecked at the Bullers o' Buchan and fifty-four perished. For the relief of the widows and children the sum of £1,300 was raised within a month.

On 9 February the Torry steam liner *Crimond* was wrecked in the Orkneys and there were no survivors. A new relief fund brought in £1,172.

The story could go on and on of the good work done in those pre-Kemsley days, but the point to stress is that still greater efforts on behalf of good causes were to be made under the new ownership. Now is a good time to take note of some of these good deeds.

There were the collections that provided the Children's Shelter in the Gallowgate. There will be memories, too, of the Girder Fund, raised just before the outbreak of the Second World War to help the victims of an accident in William Square, Aberdeen, of the Willing Shilling Fund to provide country holidays and Christmas treats for city children who might, otherwise, have been deprived of these. But perhaps the most outstanding effort of that era was that which provided war comforts for the men and women of the Forces from these parts during World War II. The War Comforts Fund was operated in conjunction with the W.V.S. through the Co-ordinated Comforts Depot in Aberdeen.

During the six years of that body's existence, of which *The Press and Journal* was the mainstay, a sum of no less than £77,143 was raised. To this figure have to be added many gifts. In point of fact, through the Depot there were distributed 200,000 razor blades, 103,655 books and magazines, 36,558 writing-pads, 20,000 tooth brushes, 818 razors, 580 footballs,

78

466 wireless sets, 427 pianos, etc. The gifts poured in following periodic appeals by *The Press and Journal.*

Linked with the war, but, happily, launched when the fighting was over, was another great *Press and Journal* effort. In October 1945, it was suggested by the newspaper that the time was ripe for a gesture of gratitude to be made by the north-east for the kindnesses paid to its sons by the inhabitants of St. Valéry-en-Caux during the last stand there, in 1940, by the 51st (Highland) Division and during the period that followed the surrender. In defiance of the Germans the men and the women and the children of St. Valéry protected our men, cared for our wounded and paid reverence to our dead. And so was launched the St. Valéry Remembrance Appeal which was to draw support from every town and village in the north-east and was ultimately to raise the sum of £8,729.

The idea behind the fund was to help, in some way, the people of St. Valéry in their task of rebuilding their shattered city. In the event, the money was devoted to the erection of a gateway to the military cemetery at St. Valéry and to the provision, at a cost of £7,500, of a Salle d'Ecosse in the new-built Council Chambers there. The granite pillars to the gateway were fashioned from Kemnay granite, while the gate itself was beautifully carved from oak grown at Aboyne.

The presentation ceremony took place on Saturday, 10 June 1950, with an inaugural address by the Marchioness of Huntly, while William Veitch handed to M. Cherfils, the Maire, a golden key with which to open the gate.

It was fitting that the ceremony should have been arranged to coincide with the unveiling of the Highland Division monument on the cliffs of St. Valéry, and many representative people from the north-east, including parents, wives and sweethearts of the fallen, were there to share in the moving spectacles. This memorial took the form of a granite monolith from Kemnay. Its transport to France, which presented special problems, was organised by *The Press and Journal.*

The list of journalistic contributions to the community's welfare is endless. To be further noted are the scholarships that enabled students of the University of Aberdeen to travel overseas and the similar arrangements on behalf of secondary pupils from an area ranging from Perth to Shetland, from the Buchan coast to the Hebrides. Pupils from fifty senior secondary schools were involved. Wherever they went they met statesmen, mayors and other V.I.P.s and, even more important, had ample opportunity to compare notes with young people of their own age.

This kind of activity is commonplace nowadays among schools and youth organisations of all kinds, but *The Press and Journal* and the *Evening Express* can claim credit for having played an important part in pioneering it.

Identification with the life of a community, such as *The Press and Journal* and the *Evening Express* have sought, presents many avenues of approach. There is little doubt that the broadest and perhaps the most direct of these relates to commercial and financial wellbeing. While striving, day by day, to further these interests, the proprietors have, from time to time, provided practical proof of their purpose.

In September 1932 an idea which had been entertained for some time took practical shape and the first Exhibition on behalf of Northern Industries, organised by *The Press and Journal*, was held. Perhaps the best proof of its value and its popularity is provided by the fact that 166,511 interested people paid for admission. The success encouraged repetition of the experiment in the following year.

The whole design was to provide a concentrated display of the industries of the area, enabling all who attended to get a comprehensive view of the means of livelihood in the area and of the sources whence it drew its wealth. It was in keeping with the idea of the exhibition that the opportunity should be taken to provide readers with practical demonstration of how their newspapers were produced.

Experience is, of course, the wisest of teachers and it was because of the lessons learned from the first exhibitions that the proprietors decided to go one better in 1935.

The need for more space had become paramount and it was to solve this problem that it was decided to erect, in 1935, a special Exhibition Hall at Kittybrewster with some 36,000 square feet of floor room. It was a project that served more than its original purpose, for the erection of the buildings did not a little towards the relief of unemployment in the city, the entire labour force being locally recruited.

The exhibition itself was featured by working models which, in fact, constituted eighty per cent of the 'show'. The doors remained open from 6 to 28 September, and once again Aberdeen and the north-east showed their appreciation of the effort of *The Press and Journal* to promote trade in its circulation area. The hall was crowded throughout the three weeks.

Other exhibitions were arranged in the years that followed, exhibitions that varied in their content and immediate appeal. There have been exhibitions voted to housing, to sport, to art and the many other activities that are part and parcel of the life of the north-east.

The point about all these activities is that, if a newspaper is to serve its area to the fullness of its powers, it must identify itself with all that is good for that area. It must not content itself with being solely a recorder of events in that area. It should play its part—a leading part—in shaping those events. This the *Journal*, in its long, long history, has unceasingly sought to do.

Chapter 12

The year 1936 was one of Royal tragedy, one in which history was made and duly recorded in the pages of *The Press and Journal* and the *Evening Express*. It was but twenty days old when the life of George V passed peacefully to its close. No one who worked then on a newspaper is likely to forget the long evening of waiting for the announcement that would completely transform the next issue. It fell to *The Press and Journal* staff to keep vigil.

George V died in the 26th year of his reign and when his eldest son, the popular Prince of Wales, succeeded him, all seemed set fair. But the year had not far advanced when the first rumblings began to be heard in newspaper offices of an association which was bound to raise difficulties with Church and State.

When, at last, it became clear that the King was not prepared to take the advice offered to him, there was but one course for him and that was to abdicate, which he did, on 11 December. He had not reigned for a year and he had never been crowned. As with the death of his father, there were anxious hours in the newspaper offices before the last word was spoken, but there was this advantage that those in authority were given sufficient advance information to cope with the situation when it actually arose.

King Edward VIII sailed from our shores and the task of kingship devolved upon his brother who had never expected that honour, with all its accompanying demands, to come his way. With the help of his Scottish Consort he humbly set about the task of restoring the lustre to the Crown which had been somewhat tarnished by the events of the year. And nobly succeeded.

And so to 1937, this to be a year, happily, of celebration and not dismay. With the Coronation fixed for 12 May, it fell to the Aberdeen newspapers to report the planning of the many festivities with which the North of Scotland wished to mark the occasion. *The Press and Journal* itself played a leading part in these by sponsoring a brilliant evening Tattoo at Pittodrie Park in which outstanding episodes in Aberdeen's history were re-enacted.

The first took onlookers back to 1222, when King Alexander II and his sister visited Aberdeen to grant a charter for the founding of a monastery to the Black Friars. The second was dated 1308 and depicted a day of battle and victory for Bruce and his Highlanders who came down from the hills to seize the Castle of Aberdeen from its English garrison.

The third took Aberdeen's story on to 1511. A fanfare heralded the arrival of Queen Margaret, Consort of James IV, a happier situation altogether, made colourful with pretty maidens, the Court jester and all the pageantry of the age. But clouds lowered again for the fourth episode, a black day for Aberdeen when the Duke of Montrose forced the Provosts of Old and New Aberdeen to carry out his demands.

The Jacobite Rising of 1715 was the subject of the fifth pageant in which wild Highlanders wrestled and leaped and townsfolk danced to mark the arrival of the Old Pretender. For the Grand Finale the enthroned figure of Britannia was picked out against the background of a gigantic Union Jack, created by massed groups of the youth organisations of the city.

The Tattoo, which was repeated on the three following nights, was made possible through the co-operation of members of the Central School F.P. Dramatic Society, of the Albyn School F.P. Dramatic Club, of the High School for Girls, of St. Katherine's Club, of the Torry Branch of the Scottish Girls' Friendly Society, of University students and of Gordon Highlanders from the depot.

1937 was an exciting and happy year, one in which the

Broad Street papers played a vital part. For a time, at least, the threat that was to rear its ugly head in 1938 held no worries—except for those permitted to see a little farther ahead than their fellows, perhaps because they were able, as is the case with newspaper men, to peer a little farther behind the scenes.

That we were living in a fool's paradise became more and more apparent as Hitler, for all his protestations that he had no more demands to make, began to turn the familiar screw on Czechoslovakia and, although some sort of peace was patched up, it became pretty evident that Neville Chamberlain's appeasement policy had produced a respite but no final settlement. And so, in 1939, it was Armageddon again.

The five years of World War II brought many problems for Broad Street, as it did for all newspapers. The young men of the staff had to go forth to war, leaving age to hold the fort, to devise and share in a system of fire-watching and to raise a unit of the Home Guard. Newsprint became more and more restricted in supply, printer's ink and all the other materials essential for newspaper production more and more difficult to obtain and transport costs kept rising.

Means of protection against bombing had to be worked out. Printing-machines had to be transferred to the basement, stretching the normal chain of production to its utmost limit and inevitably slowing down output. But never stopping it. The newspapers always came out. Most difficult problem of all, in fact, was to cover the news in the restricted space brought about by the rationing of newsprint and the increase of readership. It was a case, too, of marking time so far as plant addition and improvement were concerned. Many a scheme which had been visualised had to be shelved for the time being.

But one important change it was possible to make. On 24 April 1941, the *Evening Express* changed from 'text' to 'tabloid' size. It was a move made in the interests of the travelling public—it was easier to handle in trains and buses—and also to enable a more effective lay-out of the war news.

With the removal of newsprint restrictions and the growing volume of advertising it was decided to revert, on 10 November 1958, to the old, familiar 'text' size. Such is the effect of ingrained habit that, if there were quite a few who objected to the change, in 1941, from 'text' to 'tabloid', there were just as many with whom the reversal, in 1958, did not find favour. But all that's forgotten now.

The war years—in 1944 to be exact—were to produce another change, this time in the editorial set-up. This involved the appointment of individual editors for *The Press and Journal* and the *Evening Express*, under the over-all direction of William Veitch as Editor-in-Chief.

James M. Chalmers, who became Editor of *The Press and Journal*, had begun his journalistic career as an apprentice reader and compositor on the staff of the *Banffshire Journal* and had, later, become a sort of general factotum for the *Northern Herald* at Wick, which involved canvassing for advertisements, collecting accounts, doing a bit of clerical work, reading proofs over and above reporting. They learned the hard way in those days. At the age of twenty he had joined the *Free Press* and, after war service, had become that paper's representative for the Buchan area, with headquarters at Peterhead, a post he retained after the amalgamation. Later he returned to the head office as deputy chief reporter and by 1935 he was news editor.

George Fraser, who became Editor of the *Evening Express*, had spent all his journalistic years at Broad Street, with the exception of two on the sub-editorial staff of the *Liverpool Post*, linked very much with the north-east through the Jeans family. On his return to Aberdeen he had successively held the posts of chief sub-editor of the *Daily Journal* (later *The Press and Journal*) and of the *Evening Express*, and it was while he was serving in the latter capacity that he was promoted Editor.

Two years later a similar arrangement was made for the *Weekly Journal*, with Cuthbert Graham assuming immediate editorial control. He had joined *The Press and Journal* sub-editorial staff, just before the outbreak of World War II, from the *Bon-Accord* of which he was assistant editor.

His first task in connection with the *Weekly Journal* was to transform it from text to tabloid size. This was in May 1946. Later he was to return to *The Press and Journal* to take over control of the literary side of the paper and ultimately to produce the Saturday Review section, one of its most successful and most admired features. In proof of this one needs but mention his north-east Castles series and his broader, historical and factual illustrated surveys of the localities that constitute the North of Scotland.

But that's looking ahead quite a bit. We left a nation in the toils of war, but a war in which disaster was no longer the dominant note. Gradually it became possible to direct thoughts once more to ideas which had had to be shelved. At least ambition worked that way, but peace was to prove that it had its problems no less than war, and quite a number of moons had to wax and wane before the full tide of progress was flowing again.

First there was the build-up in staff to pre-war dimensions as a basis for further expansion in that direction. New ideas in news presentation had to be introduced, coupled with go-ahead plans for publicity and for the promotion of circulation. Plant requirements, too, had to be considered and met, particularly in the light of progress in the electrical and engineering fields as applied to the newspaper industry. Not a small part of the success of Aberdeen Journals Limited is, in fact, due to a readiness to keep well in the van of newspaper technique and mechanisation.

Chapter 13

Reference has already been made to the 200th anniversary, on Monday, 5 January 1948, of *The Press and Journal*. It could then proudly claim—and did claim—that its daily sales were far and away the largest in its history. In passing, it might be said that even the most optimistic could hardly have dared hope that it would achieve the greatly enhanced circulation of today.

One restricting influence it had to put up with at the time was the shortage of newsprint, but in the space available on that and the following day *The Press and Journal* looked back along the lengthy road it had travelled, reiterated its high principles and recorded messages of congratulation from many parts of the world—from King George VI, from the Prime Ministers of Canada, Australia, New Zealand and South Africa, from the oldest newspapers in America, Australia, New Zealand, Norway and Sweden and from the daughter towns of Aberdeen and Banff.

To mark the occasion, too, Viscount Kemsley gave a dinner to notable personalities in the public, professional, academic and ecclesiastic life of the community over and above a reception, in the Music Hall, to about 1,000 others. The Hon. Lionel Berry, Deputy Chairman of Kemsley Newspapers, presided in the unavoidable absence of Viscount Kemsley who had been invited by General Smuts to visit South Africa. Absent, too, because of illness, was the Marchioness of Huntly, but both sent messages of good wishes.

The Marquess of Aberdeen paid tribute to the manner in which *The Press and Journal* was carrying on the great traditions of the past and providing the north-east with the kind of news the public wanted.

'It started well,' he said, 'and it has continued well.' No better tribute could be paid to a newspaper than that.

Mr. William Veitch, Editor-in-Chief, underlined the point made by Lord Aberdeen. 'Under the beneficent influence of Viscount Kemsley,' he said, 'the principles which animate the whole of the staff today are the same high principles which were set by the first James Chalmers.'

Perhaps nothing brought out more dramatically the longevity of *The Press and Journal* than the pageant staged in the Music Hall. This depicted, in three episodes, the people at their pleasures at the time of the birth of the newspaper, at its centenary and at its bi-centenary. It had been largely designed and was produced by the late George Rowntree Harvey and by W. A. Mitchell of the editorial staff and performed by other employees of the firm. In addition, an exhibition of engravings, photographs and old maps marked, in different ways, the passage of time.

It was a memorable occasion and one in which the entire staff shared. Each and every one was the guest of Viscount Kemsley at a reception all to themselves. That was memorable in itself.

History does not record that champagne flowed at the inauguration ceremony 200 years earlier. Certainly the bi-centenary was well and truly toasted with well-filled glasses at the two occasions mentioned.

The year 1950 saw George E. Ley Smith, one of Aberdeen's best known journalists, succeed, as Editor of *The Press and Journal*, James M. Chalmers who had taken up an appointment at the London headquarters of Kemsley Newspapers Limited. Smith had joined the firm in 1915 at the age of fifteen. He saw service in World War I and was wounded at the Second Battle of the Marne. As a swimmer, he gained four international water-polo caps and once, while on an actual assignment to report on the shipwreck, he made a gallant effort to carry a line to a vessel stranded off the Belhelvie beaches, for which action his colleagues presented him with a gold watch.

Appointed chief reporter in 1932, he was made accredited provincial war correspondent in World War II and visited northern units in France. He also went to Norway at the liberation. In 1944 he became news editor and played a vital part in forging the links between St. Valéry and the north-east. It was for these services that he was presented, along with William Veitch and Lady Huntly, with the freedom of the town that had seen the last stand of the 51st (Highland) Division in 1940. George Smith occupied *The Press and Journal* editorial chair until 1956, when ill-health caused his retirement. His death in 1968 was greatly regretted by his old colleagues.

The pageant of newspaper history unfolds year by year, each highlighted in one way or another, but some more so than others. Such a year was 1953. It was the year of the Great Gale which devastated the woodlands of the north-east in a manner that has no parallel in the recorded history of the area.

For a time the immensity of the disaster seemed to escape Government circles and it was only when Members of Parliament were shown, in the House of Commons, the remarkable pictorial reproductions in the Aberdeen papers that authority began to take note and to do something about it.

Indeed, thanks were to come from the Forestry Commission which 'followed with admiration' the descriptions given in the Broad Street newspapers. At the same time tribute was paid for the amount of space *The Press and Journal* regularly gives to forestry matters in general.

In the spring of 1953 George Fraser was succeeded as *Evening Express* Editor by Kenneth J. Peters, his assistant editor. Peters had earlier served as an assistant editor on the Manchester *Evening Chronicle* and also worked for the *Daily Record* and *Evening News* in Glasgow. He thus returned to his native city to edit.

Coronation Day was on 2 June 1953 and celebrations in the North of Scotland took many forms. Perhaps the outstanding social event was the Coronation Ball, held in Aberdeen Beach Ballroom and attended by some 600 dancers, representative of town and county. For the occasion the ballroom was magnificently decorated, with flowers in the Coronation colours banking the approaches. Ready to give a welcome and a warm handshake were Lord and Lady Provost Graham, Lord

Aberdeen and Mr. and Mrs. William Veitch. The Lord Provost and Lord Aberdeen, along with the Lords-Lieutenant of all the counties from Angus to Caithness, were joint presidents of the ball and Mr. Veitch was chairman.

Dominating the centre of the ballroom was a magnificent crown; red, white and blue bunting draped the balcony, and shields, representing the Colonies and the Commonwealth, topped the eight pillars of the ballroom. A display, in an adjoining room, by *The Press and Journal* of wonderful reproductions of the Coronation Regalia was a tremendous source of interest. And what with side-shows and games and the high-spirited dancing it was truly a night to remember.

Coronation Day itself had proved a hectic one in newspaper production. Tremendous efforts had been made to insure complete coverage, particularly in the photographic field. In the event a continuous flow of pictures reached Broad Street by wire and altogether thirty-three of these were reproduced in the *Evening Express*. For *The Press and Journal* it had been planned to fly original prints from London to Dyce, but with fog closing in at Aberdeen Airport, that scheme had to be abandoned and the morning paper had to rely on wired pictures, thirty-nine of which were reproduced.

The quality of the pictures in both papers spoke volumes for the modern way of transmitting pictures. It is worthy of note, too, that, for the first time for fourteen years, a sixteen-page *Press and Journal* was published. To make this possible certain new rollers were required for the presses and it was thanks to Messrs. John M. Henderson and Company, Aberdeen, that these were made available in time. All the normal suppliers in the south had reported difficulties in securing the essential steel and none could guarantee delivery in time.

Two editorial appointments in 1956 should be recorded. Robert Anderson who had held that office on the *Weekly Journal*, succeeded Kenneth J. Peters as Editor of the *Evening Express*. Anderson was succeeded, as Editor of the *Weekly Journal*, by Kenneth W. McGregor who had had the distinction of being the first newspaperman in Scotland to win the Diploma of the National Council for the Training of Journalists.

There has always been time for bowls, golf, badminton, cricket or football.
The Aberdeen Journals soccer side in the 1920s

Sub-editing by candle-light. The *Press and Journal* staff at work
during a power cut in the late 1940s

The site for the seventies, eighties and beyond was selected. On the last day in the old office composing machines were loaded for transportation

Then Secretary of State for Scotland, Gordon Campbell accompanies Lord Provost James Lamond, Lord Thomson of Fleet and Mr. K. J. Peters on the opening day at Mastrick

Twenty months after the official opening of the new Mastrick premises the Queen Mother spent an afternoon touring them. In the composing-room she shared a mutual interest in flowers and fishing with Neville Myhill (*right*)

Distinguished visitors to Aberdeen Journals Ltd.: from Robert Burns to Sir John Betjeman, the Poet Laureate, seen here unveiling a plaque to commemorate the fact that Alexander Cruden, author of a noted concordance to the Bible, had previously lived in the Broad Street premises occupied by the company until 1970

The Rt. Hon. Bruce Millan, Secretary of State for Scotland studies type-setting by computerised photo-composition in 1978 in the Aberdeen Journals composing-room. Left to right: Mr. George Moncrieff, overseer; operator Mr. Alex Cruickshank; Mr. Millan and Mr. F. D. Singer, chief production manager

The giant press room of Aberdeen Journals' new plant at
Lang Stracht, Mastrick

Pipers and drummers of the 51st Highland Volunteers at the little Normandy
seaport of St. Valéry-en-Caux beside the Highland Division memorial on the
cliffs. Several pilgrimages to St. Valéry have been organised by the *Press and
Journal* which also shipped out the granite memorial

At the helm: William Veitch, editor-in-chief from 1927-57

Lord Thomson of Fleet, chairman of the company from 1959 to 1976, with K. J. Peters who edited the *Evening Express* from 1953-56, and the *Press and Journal* from 1956-60 and has been managing director from 1960

Press and Journal editors in
the 1950s, 1960s, and 1970s:
George E. Ley Smith
(1950-56) and James C. Grant
(1960-75)

Peter Watson, the present
editor appointed in 1975

George Fraser (1944-53)

Robert Anderson (1956-59)

Evening Express editors

H. R. Bawden (1959-62)

Robert Smith, the present editor
appointed in 1962

The big event of 1957 was the retirement, as Managing Director and Editor-in-Chief, of William Veitch after fifty-five years of active journalism, forty-six of them, in London and Aberdeen, with the Aberdeen papers. But, happily, he was not to sever completely his link with Aberdeen Journals Limited. As a Director he continued to serve the firm for which he had worked so long and so successfully. He was thus engaged until his death on 12 August 1968. Only a few days before he had been presented with a tie, designed shortly before, for members of the Parliamentary Press Gallery of which he had continued to be a trustee from those days, away back in 1923, when he was its chairman.

As a measure of his success it may be mentioned that, during his direction, the circulation of *The Press and Journal* rose from 25,000 to 79,000 and of the *Evening Express* from 60,000 to almost 85,000. In 1937 he was appointed a Director of Kemsley Newspapers and for four years he was President of the Scottish Daily Newspaper Society (1953–57). He was also one of the draughtsmen of the constitution of the National Council of the Press of which he became one of the three founder Scottish representatives.

In 1951 the French Government appointed him a Chevalier of the Legion of Honour. In 1955 he was made a C.B.E., while, as a Justice of the Peace, he took his place regularly on the Bench.

The passing of a newspaper, notwithstanding the overriding facts of economics, is ever a matter for regret. It was so when the *Journal* in its weekly form closed down on 1 August 1957, but the decision was inevitable, as a statement by the proprietors clearly indicated.

To produce a newspaper today entails vast outlay and, as the statement put it, comprehensive coverage each morning and evening by *The Press and Journal* and the *Evening Express* of north-east local affairs had made it problematical whether the public and advertisers could support a weekly publication devoted to the same service. Continuity had, of course, already been established through the daily morning paper and the continuous link with the founder was thus preserved. Incidentally, all the members of the *Weekly Journal* staff were given other jobs with the firm, a happy state of affairs that does not always prevail when a newspaper folds up.

Meanwhile the idea of restoring the *Evening Express* to text size had been under examination. The all-round advantages were considerable and so, on 10 November 1958, Lord Provost Stephen was invited to press the button which set in motion the first machine off which rolled the 'new look' *Evening Express*.

But, important though these changes were, there was another in the making of an even more vital order. Once more a *Journal* dynasty was moving to its close. The Chalmers regime had come and gone. So, too, had that of the Aberdeen and North of Scotland Newspaper and Printing Company. And now it was to be the parting of the ways for the Kemsley organisation.

Chapter 14

It was a good summer of 1959 in the north-east of Scotland. And in Aberdeen circles there was a predictable flavour to life in May, June and July. Midsummer and holiday activities were at their height. The fourth post-war season of drama by the Whatmore Players, under their energetic and immensely popular producer/actor Denis Ramsden, was at H.M. Theatre. Playwright John Chapman staged the world premiere of his new farce *The Brides of March* at the same venue. All was faithfully reported in the columns of *The Press and Journal* and the *Evening Express*.

The *Evening Express* had a change of editor in 1959. Robert Anderson, who had been at the editorial helm since the summer of 1956, was appointed Editor of the *Sunday Graphic*, one of the Kemsley group's national papers. He went off to his new post in London, and was succeeded in Aberdeen by H. R. Bawden, who came north from Newcastle where he had been an assistant editor, following an earlier sub-editorial spell on the Manchester *Evening Chronicle*.

But these were the only major changes in the first six months of a year which was to prove decisive in the long history of the company. Aberdeen newspaper life continued on its way, with no hint of the dramatic change of ownership to burst on not only the Granite City's newspapermen but also on morning, evening and Sunday publications the length of Britain.

Broad Street's staff knew no more than the daily round in the cosily familiar, if antiquated, straggle of buildings, on several levels, which constituted the publishing office of two daily newspapers. From time to time there had been renewed talk that 'one day' the company would move to larger premises. Plans were even drawn up of a possible enlargement of the existing site . . . more old buildings would have to be acquired first, of course, said those 'in the know'. Then such acquisitions would have to be grafted on to the existing centuries-old buildings, themselves connected by wooden corridors on roofs and doors literally hacked through brickwork. And, always, the several levels on which everyone worked . . . legacies of a head-quarters which, like Topsy, 'just growed'.

But, for the moment in the early summer of 1959, nothing like expansion was contemplated. Nor was change of owner-ship! Nor was any problem of the company's viability. Circu-lations of both papers had expanded. The morning paper was nearing a sale of 90,000 copies a day; its sister evening paper had a healthy daily sale of 80,000. What else seemed to matter, might have been the argument? Broad Street's cosiness and the big, rather ramshackle family chain of Kemsley Newspapers seemed secure and safe from the occasional blasts of adverse economic winds which affected other papers in the South.

Out of a clear, blue, July sky, therefore, came the first rumours. Someone was trying to buy Kemsley Newspapers. 'And that would also mean us in Broad Street', said members of the *Journals'* staff.

The now-famous deal between Lord Kemsley and Scots-Canadian Roy Thomson was planned and worked at in July. By 14 August, an extraordinary general meeting at the Gray's Inn Road headquarters of Kemsley Newspapers, gave Roy Thomson the whole of the Kemsley empire. Roy Thomson, it was announced, would take control on 23 August. The two Aberdeen papers would thus have a new owner . . . although they were to remain in the company of so many others up and down these islands. They were also to gain new Scottish cousins in the *Scotsman* and the *Evening Dispatch* in Edinburgh.

What did it all mean, Broad Street's newspapermen asked themselves? What kind of man is this Roy Thomson? Edin-burgh's *Scotsman* staff could tell them. Some who knew mem-bers of the Aberdeen staff did. Alastair Dunnett, then Editor of the *Scotsman* and a former boss of Aberdeen's *Press and Journal*

Editor at the time, K. J. Peters, rang his old employee in Broad Street.

'You're going to like working for Roy', said West Highlander Dunnett who had himself been hired by Thomson when the Mirror group bought Dunnett's old paper, the *Daily Record* from Kemsley towards the end of 1955. 'He understands local papers: you'll get a lot of freedom. He's really enthusiastic about owning the Aberdeen papers now that he has bought out Kemsley. In fact he always wanted Aberdeen', added the *Scotsman* chief.

And a story then came out which both startled and even flattered many folk working for Aberdeen Journals Ltd. It transpired that even in his Canadian days, Roy Thomson had wanted to purchase a British local newspaper company. And the one he fancied was Aberdeen Journals Ltd. Twice, it seemed, he had tried to buy the two North of Scotland daily papers. Things ran this way: seven years earlier, in 1952, Roy Thomson had stated, at a Press conference in London, that he was not averse to owning some local papers in the U.K. Shortly afterwards, he discussed the possibility of purchasing Aberdeen Journals Ltd. A price of £2m. was put on the Aberdeen papers, where Lord Kemsley's only daughter, the Marchioness of Huntly, was a director of the company. Roy Thomson grasped the point at once. 'At £2m. the Aberdeen papers are not really for sale', he commented to Kemsley's Editorial Director who quoted to him the asking price of the then Gray's Inn Road newspaper baron.

In the spring of 1959, Thomson tackled Lord Kemsley again about the possibility of purchasing Aberdeen Journals. This time the Kemsley price was upped to £2,500,000. Roy Thomson, who knew about balance sheets and profits as well as any newspaper tycoon in this world, reckoned the falling Aberdeen profits could not support such a price tag, and realised again that really Aberdeen's two papers were not for sale.

Yet, in a matter of weeks, they had passed to him in the whole, giant Kemsley package which was bought by the chunky Canadian-Scot with the penetrating eyes behind the thick glasses. Aberdeen's newspaper folk hadn't known at the time of the two previous bids for their papers—seven years apart. It was the second take-over of the company in forty-one years. Understandable, initial nervousness on the part of staff gave way later in the autumn to a sense of shock when the new owners made it known that an examination of the financial state of Aberdeen Journals Ltd. had not exactly inspired confidence in the future. The Thomson Group's Deputy Managing Director, Eric Cheadle, visited Aberdeen. He was well-known in the newspaper world and had been Kemsley's Circulation Director. He knew well several of the Aberdeen executives.

He met managers and he met representatives of the trade unions in the office. He sat at the Board Room table with them and he outlined patiently the problems and what might be done to get the Aberdeen company into a healthy financial condition. He pointed out something the staff had never guessed: the morning paper had been losing a lot of money over the past few years. The time had come, revealed Eric Cheadle, when the *Evening Express*, which had for a long time earned more profit than the morning paper, could no longer carry, financially, its 'elder brother'.

The early months of 1960, therefore, saw vigorous action on all sides to enable *The Press and Journal* to pay its way and, thus, to permit the company to trade at a profit. Staffs were informed of what was needed; they responded to both the confidence and the investment of Roy Thomson, who had, typically and colourfully expressed himself to his Aberdeen staff, during an interview in London: 'Can't you good guys up there live like Aberdonians? That way, you'll save your papers and your jobs.'

The Aberdonians took his point. Their jobs and their papers gradually looked more and more secure as 1960 progressed. They buckled to, and a great deal of waste (much of it had never fully been appreciated) was eliminated in a drive to make Aberdeen's two papers into the lasting, confident, profitable publications Roy Thomson and the staffs felt they should be.

Changes in command came along . . . but gradually. And it was to the local talent that Roy Thomson and his executives turned.

Former general manager John Noble had joined the Corporation of the City of Aberdeen where he headed the 'internal audit' department, and where he was to serve his adopted city for the next fourteen to fifteen years.

William Pattillo, the chief accountant and long-serving secretary of the Girder Disaster Trust Fund (which Aberdeen Journals Ltd. had initiated twenty years earlier) was promoted to Company Secretary. He had just recruited from the company's local auditors, a young accountant, William Forsyth (no relation of the former editor), and Forsyth was to become, successively, chief accountant, assistant general manager and then assistant managing director.

He began, then, in the last days of 1959, a long association with the newly-appointed general manager (shortly afterwards to be confirmed as managing director), K. J. Peters, who had edited *The Press and Journal* since spring 1956 and then moved over to the top management chair. To succeed him as Editor, the paper's deputy editor, James C. Grant, a native of Elgin, stepped up, to remain Editor until 1975, a period of continuity in editing not often witnessed in far-off Fleet Street.

James Grant had joined the reporting staff of Aberdeen Journals Ltd. in 1936, and had represented the firm in both Edinburgh and Glasgow before serving in the Royal Artillery from the outbreak of World War II. After six years' service, he returned to Aberdeen as a sub-editor, to become, successively, assistant editor and deputy editor before being appointed as editor in early 1960.

In later 1961, *Evening Express* editor H. R. Bawden moved to the *Sunday Times* before returning to an executive post on his native Merseyside and a distinguished career with the BBC. He was succeeded in the *Evening Express* editor's chair by Robert Smith who had been his deputy. Again, there began a lengthy period of stability and continuity in editing. Robert Smith, another local man, had learned the newspaper craft both in Aberdeen and Dundee. He was still in the chair as the paper's centenary in 1979 approached. During World War II he had served with the R.A.F.

The company then set out on its march into the 1960s, a

decade of change and trauma for all British newspapers . . . not just in Aberdeen. The Board of the parent company, now called Thomson, instead of Kemsley, Newspapers, reflected the major change of ownership. Lord and Lady Kemsley had resigned from the board and the remaining members of the family withdrew on 6 November 1959. The name of the parent company itself was changed on the previous day to Thomson Newspapers Limited, but no alteration was made in the title of Aberdeen Journals Ltd. which carried on, with Roy H. Thomson, James M. Coltart and William Veitch as directors. Later they were to be joined by Kenneth J. Peters (March 1961) and William J. Pattillo (February 1962), and Harry Robertson at the end of the sixties. Pattillo retired from his posts as Chief Accountant and Company Secretary in 1963 while retaining his directorship. He had 'come over' from the *Free Press* at the time of the amalgamation and had succeeded William Ogg as cashier on his death in 1931. Promoted Chief Accountant in 1943, he became Company Secretary on 1 January 1960.

The whirligigs of time can produce amusing, as well as strange, situations. Perhaps the older men of Aberdeen Journals Ltd. smiled a wry little smile at the time of the Thomson take-over as they recalled a leading article in the *Evening Dispatch* at the time when the Berry Brothers acquired the Aberdeen papers. It is, indeed, never very wise to be over-righteous in judgment. It is an attitude that can come home to roost. The *Dispatch* related the circumstances concerning the sale of the Aberdeen newspapers and went on to say:

> It must be regretted by all who are solicitous for what is best in Scottish life that Aberdeen has gone over to the 'enemy' . . .
>
> The independence of the Scottish Press is being rapidly eroded, a development that will subtly and adversely react upon the whole national life. Every true Scot must regret the capitulation of the granite citadel of the North, which furnishes another milestone in the onward march of Anglification.

Of course it didn't work out that way under the Kemsley

regime; and it might be added here that the 'march of Anglification', which was never much in evidence, if at all, under Lord Kemsley, most assuredly became a retreat under Roy Thomson who himself set the seal on that when he issued a personal statement at the time of the deal. As he put it:

'The newspapers of the group published outside London serve some of the most important and flourishing regions in Britain.

'Each of these papers—including *The Press and Journal*—has, for many years, played an important role in the communal life of its area, recording, interpreting and influencing, and nowhere more so than in the North of Scotland.

'I shall ensure, so far as I can, that these papers will not only continue to play that role, but will be encouraged and supported in expanding and developing it so that they may keep pace with—and, indeed, lead—the expansion and development of their communities.

'The primary responsibility rests with the Editors, and it has always been my policy to give them the greatest possible freedom of action to further the interests of their communities and papers.'

And that, let it be said, has been editorial experience from the word 'go'.

Expansion had been the keyword during the Kemsley regime. It had been realised in circulation, mechanisation, in staffing increases—editorial, production and commercial. There had been considerable changes in accommodation, making for better all-round facilities.

A further practical development was the overhaul of the library system, largely undertaken by Peter H. Tough, a graduate of Aberdeen University, who had previously been in charge of the Features Department. To his new task he brought a meticulous care and a tidiness of mind that set a standard for those who succeeded him.

And, finally, it should be noted that it was Lord Kemsley who introduced the happy idea of awarding gold watches to long-service employees, a practice which Lord Thomson continued while reducing the number of years of qualification.

Chapter 15

One of the aspects of the management of two important daily Scottish newspapers which required some attention in early 1960 was community involvement and the establishment of a climate in which the marketing of Aberdeen's two papers and their advertising services could satisfactorily take place.

With the retirement of William Veitch, and then two years later the long summer of the 1959 take-over with its successive uneasiness and doubts about the future, not enough time could and had been spared to the P.R. aspects of the Company's work. Before he retired in the spring of 1957, William Veitch had been a man at the centre of many aspects of public life and community involvement. It was almost inevitable that a period of re-adjustment and change would follow a man who had reigned over the affairs and fortunes of Aberdeen Journals Ltd. for thirty years.

The Thomson take-over, then, in 1959's summer, was followed by a not-unexpected vacuum in the P.R. relationship between the company and its north-east community. News, of course, flowed into the reporting room, to be printed in the columns of *The Press and Journal* and *Evening Express* with as much editorial gusto and flair as ever. But many in responsible posts in Broad Street as well as the firm's advertisement representatives found a polite, but temporary coolness on the part of the public—both readers and customers. Caution, too, as the autumn wore on, for little attention could be paid in November and December to public relations.

Early in the New Year, the fashioning of the first management budget (1960) within the framework of which the company would operate took place. George Pratt, a genial, bluff but shrewd Englishman who presided over the Group's Middlesbrough office, came to Aberdeen, along with W. H. Pearey of the Gray's Inn Road, London office. With the newly-appointed general manager, company secretary and W. P. Forsyth, who had just joined the accountancy function from the company's auditors, they slogged through punishing days of intense work, extending often into the long reaches of the night, until departmental figures and forecasts began to look a bit healthier—usually in the wee sma' oors of a post-midnight session.

The time came to consider public relations. Roy Thomson's managing director from London, James M. Coltart who hailed from Clydeside, was due to visit the office. And he was to be accompanied by the editorial director, Denis Hamilton—himself no stranger to the Granite City. The general manager tackled the leading citizens and public figures of the area. And they responded by turning up to a significant lunch party to meet the visitors from London and the new team in Broad Street. Lord Provost, university principal, chief constable, business, commercial and administrative leaders discussed Broad Street affairs round the table, with their hosts, touching more than somewhat on the future of both papers and whether they could be saved financially. They all seemed genuinely pleased and relieved when the two directors from London's Gray's Inn Road assured them that early indications confirmed that the Thomson investment in Aberdeen was neither being wasted nor was it unnecessary. They said the same things, equally pointedly, to staff gatherings in the rather cramped board room in Broad Street. And the staff breathed more easily and began to see the way ahead.

One of the Company's long-standing post-war charity enterprises—the link with the little French seaport of St. Valéry—was resumed in 1960, when the firm, in conjunction with civic and military leaders in the north-east and the Highlands of Scotland, organised another pilgrimage to the scene of the 1940 capture by the German forces of the 51st Highland Division.

Now the company started to expand: both its influence and its staff numbers began to grow in harmony with increasing activity. Just three years earlier it had been a small-sized operation with much regard for the control and influence of its chief, who set its policy within the adaptably easy and rather loose reins of the old Kemsley Empire. Decisions were made largely in his office . . . salary increases, where considered justified, were arranged in a cosy, but sometimes delightfully intimate way.

Staff had access to a managing director, mellowed with age and years of experience in the newspaper game. A manager would be with him for instructions, for about twenty minutes. He would emerge from the holy of holies, carefully shutting the big, heavy, wooden door behind him, only to see the office boy brush past him brightly, knock once and march into the managing director's presence on a particular point about which he had previously booked an appointment.

And, in the 'wings', a distraught chief sub-editor, page plans and proofs in his hand, waited impatiently to consult the boss (who was also editor-in-chief) on a matter of policy and emphasis in the editorial columns of the paper then in production and hastening remorselessly towards deadline time and first edition printing minute.

A nervous glance sideways at the dictatorial clock . . . another cigarette. And then, almost at the eleventh hour, the chief sub, shrugging off earlier indecision, pushed open the chief's door, to try to cut short the interview which the office boy had sought and got. 'The paper's about to go to press,' he would cut in, hoping to gain the chief's approval of the line he had already taken . . .

Big changes were about to take place as one by one, older members of the staff thought about retiring. These were the men and women who had, in the main, carried Aberdeen's papers through the demandingly difficult days of nearly six years of World War II and the decade which followed. Some could and should have retired by 1960. Many weren't sure how to go about things, and, indeed, sixty-five didn't really mean much as an age to take things a little more easily when so many worked on, in the company, into their seventies. But more and more were finding the going harder in the evening of long careers of service, all with Aberdeen Journals Ltd., that they plucked up courage to ask about retirement.

The new chief and his senior executives had ideas. And it was to Mr. W. P. (Bill) Forsyth that the new managing director of the sixties turned for a general policy to be put into practice. Henceforth, a man or woman had a chat, a year before normal retirement date, about the future and how he or she saw it. Nobody was compelled to go, and, as a result, most chose, at normal retiring time, to take well-earned leisure.

Inevitable and impressive, too, that, as some of the last over sixty-five age group came to retirement, one man broke all records for his length of service with Aberdeen Journals Ltd. Peter Bird, compositor and linotype operator, had commenced work with the firm in 1901, shortly after Queen Victoria died. After sixty-one years in harness, and with the congratulatory words of Mr. Kenneth R. Thomson (afterwards, Lord Thomson of Fleet) ringing in his ears, Peter Bird retired, having established a record not likely in modern times to be broken.

And, as many of the 'old faithfuls' went into retirement and handed on the newspaper torch to the youngsters succeeding them, the company refused to consider that the new (and old) pensioners had severed their connections with Broad Street (and, in later years, Mastrick). A retired staff club was formed. All the company's pensioners were automatically made members. Managing director and retired managing director planned it out one night, the latter being deputed to take charge. An annual dinner was launched; a pre-Christmas visit to the office, with a gala tea-party was instituted. Christmas cards and calendars were sent to the members. And copies of the newly-launched house magazine (*Free Press*—an artfully evocative title, that) were posted to them all.

By the seventies, in addition, a summer coach run, with high tea en route, was substituted for the earlier dinner, and members of the retired staff thronged the coach. The total membership, by the approach of the *Evening Express* centenary, had exceeded 120.

A new management structure, tailored to the sixties, evolved. A team took the reins, with heads of departments responsible

103

to the managing director for the running of the office. By the time the seventies dawned, the team had streamlined to two assistant managing directors, the two editors, the chief production manager, the personnel and training officer and the company secretary/chief accountant—all with the managing director. And that was the style of management which suited most the modernised old company which was searching for new heights in the seventies and eighties, with over 200 years of experience backing the investment in the future and the year 2000.

But before the new style had fully evolved, there were more milestones to be passed. Both papers had slogged their ways out of the financial bog which threatened them in the mid and late fifties. Now, in 1961, 1962 and 1963, they were able, for the first time in a decade, to peer cautiously to the future and to contemplate growth from being a very small-sized newspaper group to a medium-large, two-paper centre, with its morning and evening publications being able to speak more and more definitely for the north-east and the Highlands . . . two spokesmen, as it were, for the northern half of Scotland.

Chapter 16

Over 600 were now employed; the retired staff 'club' was growing; a marketing presentation, in a plush setting at a London Park Lane Hotel, was mounted in 1963. Roy Thomson (one year afterwards to be created the first Lord Thomson of Fleet) hosted the big occasion, attended by dozens of newspaper chiefs, London agency heads, the Professor of Political Economy at Aberdeen University (who had taken an enormous interest in the survey and the presentation and had written at length in *The Press and Journal*) and one or two of Aberdeen's top management team who almost didn't believe that, four short years after being warned that a key might have to be turned in the lock of the office door to close it forever, here they were, showing off two, successful Scottish daily papers to the media-men of London.

Progress, then, was steady, if not spectacular. 1964 was planned to continue cautiously and without undue pressure or haste.

That was before Aberdeen's typhoid outbreak! Out of a clear blue Aberdeen sky (or, rather, out of corned beef tins) came an infection which hospitalised almost 500 cases.

The Granite City had never known anything like it. Individual cases were stunning and worrying. And, behind them all, was the fear of a great city, usually regarded as one of the United Kingdom's cleanest, most glittering, open townships with proud buildings and wide streets.

Unclean with typhoid? Aberdeen? It seemed unthinkable. But the total of cases mounted. And the city's medical officer of health issued solemn warning after solemn warning. Fear indeed did attack a city. People were told: don't come out to crowd public places and restaurants, keep away from dance-halls. In effect, they were warned: stay at home. And keep clean—wash your hands at every opportunity. National newspapers and magazines took up the grim tale. And added to it. 'People are dying in the streets', shrieked strident U.S. newspaper and magazine headlines. Other overseas publications printed special reports of a city panicking with the disease. 'From our own special reporter in the typhoid-stricken Granite City', they trumpeted.

Against this background, Broad Street's *Press and Journal* and the *Evening Express* maintained a calm, and difficult-to-maintain balance in their reporting, day by day, the progress of the outbreak and the steps being taken by the authorities to combat it. And, by their calm, balanced, unspectacular and unsensational approach, the two local papers played, in their own community, one of their most significant roles in many years. And the 'locals' pitted traditional and knowledgeable local know-how against the 'foreigners'.

But accurate and balanced reporting was only one side of the coin. The number of cases by mid-May had not fallen. And nobody was coming to Aberdeen. Trading and business, in and out of Aberdeen, was at a low level. Civic leaders, Chamber of Commerce chiefs and trade union officials began to fear heavy unemployment. Threats of pay-offs mounted.

Then, one Monday morning the city's respected, new Lord Provost, Norman Hogg, himself a trade union organiser, and who had been in office for only a few weeks but whose friendly but firm leadership had been quickly in evidence, called the Chamber of Commerce's equally new president, Mr. James C. Williamson and Aberdeen Journals' managing director to a meeting with him at the Town House, headquarters of the city's administration. He revealed his sincere and worried fear of the fact that business was at a standstill and that he feared heavy unemployment. The city's medical officer of health, he revealed, had assured him that the number of typhoid cases had peaked, and that the medical authorities felt the worst was over. Could this new fact be conveyed to business circles and to the public?

James Williamson himself head of a noted North of Scotland wholesaling firm as well as being the Chamber of Commerce's chief, and the Journals' managing director assured him of support. And off they went to translate words into action.

The medical men had correctly assessed the situation. With the Chamber of Commerce's help, and the co-operation of the trade unions in spreading the message of confidence, both local papers probed, reported and re-assured in their publishing of new figures, new trends—and new hope. The picture began to change . . .

But still people didn't come to what had been described elsewhere as 'the stricken city'. It needed something more dramatic: a gesture was required. Colourful and positive, it must be. Hints were dropped in certain circles. And, on the Royal yacht *Britannia*, off the Scottish coast, the Queen's decision, on a Friday, was to visit the city at once, reaching it on the Royal train on the following Saturday night.

When the total surprise had been absorbed by Town House officials, instant action was ordered. And, late on the Saturday during an evening of sunlit splendour, the Queen drove slowly from the station to the Castlegate, through streets packed with cheering folk. Inside the Town House, at a reception for those who had fought and beaten typhoid, the Queen met the men and women responsible for weeks of work and ultimate triumph.

Then she emerged . . . to a tumultuous roar of welcome from massed thousands. Aberdonians, it is said, seldom show emotion towards Royal visitors. They broke their habit that night. It was a film-star acclamation Her Majesty received, as once again the car inched its way through the narrowest of lanes left by waving, cheering spectators.

Back at the station, she paused, on boarding the Royal train, to say a last word to Lord Provost Hogg. He mentioned something of the over-exuberance of the crowds who had swarmed round her car. 'Don't worry, Lord Provost', the Queen replied, 'now I know what it's like to be like the Beatles'—a Royal reference to the immense current popularity of the then bill-topping Liverpool quartet.

On the Monday, the two local papers reported the Royal night. Aberdeen was 'clean' again. The Queen had demonstrated this to the world. And the city picked itself up. And the first business visitors arrived again—to find a successful summer show running at His Majesty's Theatre. Andy Stewart had opened, despite typhoid. And he packed them in.

With the Aberdeen typhoid outbreak in the past, the company continued to strive to increase its sphere of influence, augment the sales of its two papers and to improve its share of advertising in the Highlands and the north-east of Scotland.

National morning papers, printed in Glasgow, Manchester and London, for long had supplied the main opposition to *The Press and Journal* in the battle for circulation sales, and also in the sphere of national advertising. Since the end of World War II, they had stepped up the pace of their rivalry, and most of them ensured that they were available early in the morning each day at Aberdeen, to try to offset the company's morning paper in its long-established achievement in offering the latest news earliest in the morning.

The *Scottish Daily Express* and the re-vamped *Daily Record* (now under *Daily Mirror* ownership) offered the sternest challenge in the 1963/64 era. They were vigorous with their rivalry. Money appeared no object when these two papers, in particular, considered it necessary—as they often did—to add more reporters and more photographers to those already stationed in Aberdeen on their behalf. The same liberality took place if extra motor vans or extra copies of their papers were considered essential in the bid to flood Aberdeen and the north-east with papers printed far from Buchan and the Granite City.

In 1963, too, there appeared on the scene yet another competitor . . . both for advertising revenue and for the leisure time of the folk of the North of Scotland. Grampian Television Ltd., housed in new buildings custom-built on the site of an old tramway depot in Fountainhall Road, Aberdeen, made its bow as the then I.T.V.'s most northerly station. Small, in comparison with most of the other commercial T.V. stations, it was strident and, very quickly, confident. Its programmes, other than the networked features, were couthy and local largely to the Aberdeen environment.

Its advertising, most of a national flavour at the outset, nevertheless meant that it 'hooked on' to the commercial network for the big campaigns.

The whole advent of Grampian T.V. served to remind the Company that it enjoyed no monopoly of advertising, or of people's leisure time, in fact. Aberdeen Journals Ltd. had never believed that it enjoyed any prescribed right to such ... so competition, healthy and vigorous, did not take it too much by surprise.

Meanwhile, in another direction, the Company was gradually re-establishing some of the lost influence the Company had previously enjoyed. Some years earlier, the managing director had become a member of a national Scottish Week Committee, based in Edinburgh. He now became vice-chairman of its Publicity Committee, as well as being elected a Rotarian. But in the strictly professional world of the Scottish Daily Newspaper Society, the governing body of the Scottish morning, evening and Sunday newspaper world, he had been a member since the early days of 1960.

In 1964, he was named president of that body for two years ... the second Aberdeen Journals Ltd. man to hold this office. William Veitch had chaired the Society during World War II. K. J. Peters was to be re-elected for a further term of president in the years 1974–76. Other senior members of the Company's staff served in the fifties, sixties and seventies on the various sub-committees—advertising, circulation and editorial ... and also on the more recently-established Labour and General Purposes Committees in the seventies.

Involvement, also developed in the north-east and in Scottish affairs as the sixties progressed. The company was concerned with, and participated in, the Girder Disaster Fund Trust, and the link with the little French town of St. Valéry. It was represented in Edinburgh on the Scottish Council for Development and Industry; the British Council's Scottish Advisory Committee and the Publicity Committee of the Commonwealth Games, held in Auld Reekie.

It joined membership of the senior and junior Chambers of Commerce in Aberdeen; the Business and Professional Club and, in both Edinburgh and London, the National Council for the Training of Journalists. It was invited to serve on the Films of Scotland Committee and the managing director was named vice-chairman of the Publicity Committee of the Church of Scotland in Edinburgh. The offices of president, chairman and secretary of the Publicity Club of Aberdeen have all, in the 1960s and 1970s, been held by executives of the company, and the managing director was elected to the board of the Aberdeen Association of Social Services in the 1970s, also joining the Press Council. Peters, made a JP in the early 1960s, was, in 1978, commissioned as a Deputy Lieutenant of Aberdeen—first member of staff to be honoured thus.

Aberdeen Journals Ltd. played a major part in the launching of, and participation in, the Festival of Bon-Accord, a midsummer fiesta of holidaytime events in the city which had been born in the summer of typhoid, as an attempt to pick up the city and its visitors after that scourge. The Festival survived to be an annual part of the Granite City's summer calendar, with the Company co-sponsoring it along with Aberdeen Junior Chamber.

The scope and activities of both papers increased in harmony. But Broad Street 'bulged', although occasionally, as staff members and executives went off on residential courses, there would be a spare seat and perhaps even a spare desk for their deputies to sit down to work while the 'boss' was away ... Residential management courses (one week and two weeks) took place in the sixties and seventies at such diverse places as the Universities of Oxford and Strathclyde. Ashridge Management College, too, claimed a growing number of students from the ranks of management in Aberdeen Journals Ltd.

Industrial relations activities in the office grew, with more complexities and shorter durations of agreements between the various unions and the Company.

More promotions took place, and these usually came from within the office. Occasionally, especially in the editorial and advertisement departments, there were infusions of new blood.

On the commercial side, and as part of the development of people in the Thomson Regional Newspapers group, a succession of executives took place, to direct advertising, circulation and promotions.

Elis Evans and Roy Pritchard, both Welshmen who had served in Thomson's Cardiff office, held office in charge of the commercial function. So did Englishman David Fennell and Scots Ian Colledge and Roger Nicholson, all of whom had, also, co-incidentally, served at one time during their careers, in the Cardiff office 'training ground'. Roger Nicholson, a former journalist and M.P. in Rhodesia, took over as assistant managing director (Commercial) in the early seventies, to make a profound mark, with personality and ability, as the oil era dawned.

But the mid-sixties were witnessing fast growth in the company's influence, activities and even in the depth of experience and knowledge by managers and supervisors in the various departments. The old Broad Street office was now packed with people. It had never been designed for the mid-twentieth century, and it was now a labyrinth of dark corridors, makeshift rooms (often with no windows, and only 'borrowed ventilation'). Massive, heavy and often out-of-date machinery stood side by side with modern, electronic equipment. More and more such equipment was coming in, and was due to arrive. Floors needed to be strengthened, new doors knocked through walls. The sub-editors' room was doubled in length; the board room was stripped of its former glory and split into two rooms for advertisement representatives. Three members of the senior management team lived in small rooms with little light . . . one with no windows at all. And these three rooms existed where only one had been previously. It was all make-do and mend.

Chapter 17

Outside the office, the narrow Broad Street was created a one-way thoroughfare. Double yellow lines were painted, but still the company was obliged to park heavy lorries outside its premises, thereafter to roll its reels of newsprint from those lorries. Down slipways rumbled the reels to the surface of a cobbled street. Then they had to be manhandled up a narrow alleyway to a press room away to the rear of the building.

Yet the sun shone through tall windows on a large and well-equipped department, described by a visiting London director as the most luxurious newspaper library outside *The Times*. This was a high compliment, but to a staff, hard-pressed to find space for themselves and their equipment, it was, perhaps, a rueful one. Because now, the space and equipment restrictions began to bite deeply. Both papers were finding it difficult to expand as they required. It was becoming more and more difficult and troublesome to print the larger sizes of newspapers, or to increase the number of copies required, the way the sixties, seventies and beyond were demanding. Other daily papers had led the way with larger sizes: Aberdeen Journals Ltd. was finding its faithful, but ageing, equipment beginning to be a handicap. The problems had changed. A team had been built up, and skilled staff abounded. More news was flowing in, and more advertising. The firm was no longer a small, side-street affair. It needed space, new equipment and a more modern outlook.

Once again, the rumour was heard: we're going to move. Once again, nobody on the staff believed it. 'We're going across the road, opposite Marischal College—just up Broad Street', ran one well-informed rumour. 'No we're not: we're taking

over the building which currently houses the Students' Union.'
Another story ran round the building: 'We're going into the
buildings above Jamieson & Carry, the jeweller, on Union
Bridge.'

One enterprising staff member got nearer the truth than he
ever realised, when he said: 'We're staying right where we are.
We'll put on a new frontage, but basically we'll be as we are,
and we'll stay here in our narrow old thoroughfare called
Broad Street.' His was a shrewd guess. There *had* been just
such a scheme. And preliminary plans had actually been
prepared . . . which would even require the altering of the
width of the east pavement of Broad Street. But what was
proposed, when the Company took a look at these plans which
had been drawn up some years before, was really only a face-
lift. Certainly, the front part of the old collection of buildings
was to be tidied up and improved. But, sadly, the drawings did
not reveal any increased allowance for the desperately required
space to house better equipment and space to instal modern
presses—and even access to such.

Then someone came up with the ingenious idea of acquiring
the south side of an adjoining thoroughfare, Queen Street, at
that time merely a drab collection of old shops and dwelling-
houses backing on to the machine-room of the company. Pull
down the old shops, ran the argument. Erect new, administrative offices, etc. for us . . . and the work can proceed while
we stay in our old site in Broad Street. Then we can link the
two buildings.

It was worth considering. Indeed, talks took place between
the Managing Director, the then Town Clerk and the then
Lord Provost of Aberdeen, Dr. George Stephen. These were
friendly, amicable discussions, totally unlike the ones of some
years before, which had opened and closed abruptly in five
minutes—never to be resumed.

What was obvious this time, however, was that the whole
area of Broad Street and Queen Street was not scheduled for
commercial development. Sadly, Aberdeen Journals Ltd. had to
absorb this fact. Into the bargain, Aberdeen Town Council
were keen to acquire the Journals' site to proceed with the

extension of their own municipal buildings, and to encourage the total redevelopment of the Broad Street/Queen Street area into a new complex. And this was only a question of time, in their minds . . .

Once more, the Company looked round. And this look round was at last decisive and fruitful. With the help of the civic authorities, it was agreed that Aberdeen Journals Ltd. would construct a brand-new building on the Corporation's Mastrick Industrial Estate, about three miles west of the existing site, and in a much more open, less congested area of the city . . . with access to one of the main thoroughfares, running north and south, connecting with towns and cities in both directions.

The then Lord Provost, the Rev. Professor John Graham, and the managing director signed the agreement. Broad Street's days as a newspaper headquarters were numbered, although there were hundreds on the staff who refused to believe that there was going to be a move, claiming that 'they'd heard it all before'. This time, however, it all began to happen. The new area was examined . . . soil tests carried out . . . plans drawn and meetings convened, both in Aberdeen and London. 'Operation Mastrick' was being planned in the late sixties, and, at the start of 1969, building work commenced on the site. Project managers from the staff were appointed; a project engineer came north from London office.

The shape of things to come were there for all to see, as the great grey building arose on the industrial estate where once the famous firm of Cockers grew their roses. The Hon. Kenneth R. Thomson (afterwards the second Lord Thomson of Fleet) came to inspect the progress, after the preliminary work had been done by Jenkins & Marr, the company's long-term local architects and James Shankley, the Aberdeen surveyor. Meanwhile, the Broad Street site was sold to Aberdeen Town Council, and by the summer of 1970, an extraordinary feat began to be performed daily: the company was printing in two places at once, three miles apart. The first of the giant presses had been stripped down and re-assembled at Mastrick. By midsummer, 1970, it was doing duty once more, printing in the new building. So was a 'pivot' press in Broad Street. It came into use to allow the second of the existing presses, destined for Mastrick, to be stripped down at Broad Street and rebuilt in the new home. By the autumn of that year, both presses were in position, side by side, ready to run in harmony. So the great move of three miles was planned to take place one weekend in the autumn. It was the most unusual assignment ever tackled by a famous old company and its staff.

Papers could not cease publication. So, it was arranged that, after the end of printing the Green Final edition of the *Evening Express* one Saturday night at Broad Street, the linotype machines and other composing equipment would be craned out of Broad Street's cramped old quarters . . . as would other equipment necessary to be in Broad Street to the last minute, including the electronic telegraph machines. All of this equipment would be sent on low loaders for the three-mile journey to the new Mastrick headquarters.

Helped by meticulous planning and organisation, office furniture, filing cabinets, library pictures and cuttings, editorial desks and cupboards and typewriters were all secured and labelled, department by department. Precious possessions were assured of safe delivery 'at the other end' . . . to the exact spot in the new area, marked on a plan. One or two of the company's historic clocks had to be moved very carefully indeed, especially the 'grandfather' which had gone into service in 1769 and which nobody on the staff had any intention of allowing to go into retirement, just because of a move. Reverently and with great care, it was moved to Mastrick, and established in its new place of honour where it ticked away as merrily as ever. The handsome and ornate table clock, built by the Aberdeen firm of George Jamieson (forerunner of the modern Jamieson & Carry) had adorned the Broad Street board room for years. Now, covered securely with a blanket, it was guarded in the back seat of his car by the wife of the managing director, as it made its journey westwards to its new home.

The whole weekend move was a triumph. In the dying hours of Saturday night, while some of the journalists on the staff played hosts to a farewell party in Broad Street, other journalists and their colleagues from other departments were journeying, in cars, lorries and low-loaders to Mastrick, supervising the arrival of the linotype machines, helping them into position and welcoming the operators who, not long after midnight on the Saturday, were sitting at their own, particular machines, tapping out type for Monday's *Press and Journal*, the first of the two papers to be produced, in entirety, in the new office.

Transportation was not without its hazards. It had been a mild and open autumn to date, but on that Saturday night there took place the first keen frost of the winter. Lorries and low-loaders, nearing the new office at the top of the hill at the western end of Westburn Road, found themselves skidding on a glassy surface. Sand had to be obtained—and brought to the junction of Western Road and Anderson Drive, as quickly as possible, to get the low-loaders moving again. The many vehicles involved in the move went very warily, in view of the frost—the only icy conditions, as it subsequently turned out, of the autumn.

The work of the gigantic move went on through the Saturday night and through the Sunday, and when, on Sunday night, the preparation of Monday's *Press and Journal* culminated with the running of both presses around midnight, quite a gathering of staff cheered the birth of the new era. A new office was being hanselled, and a new canteen was open, with meals and coffees and teas being consumed through the nights of Saturday and Sunday.

Canteen? Broad Street had never known anything like that. Overnight, a new meeting-place had been established, and new contacts and friendships were able to be forged over the inevitable teas, coffees and hot meals.

By the Monday morning, staff in the various departments were examining their new homes, unpacking files and possessions, and arranging where everyone was to sit. Like a family entering a new house, much of the settling down process was a case of trial and error, until everyone had absorbed the new areas, and the new atmosphere. There were new neighbours, also. In Mastrick, in an industrial estate, the staff found firms around them, bearing well-known names, and all interested to see the newcomer to the estate, Aberdeen Journals Ltd. On the social side, it was goodbye to the changing environment of Aberdeen's quaintly-named Broad Street, with its disappearing narrow lanes at the back of Union Street, and the reducing number of once-famous pubs. New hostelries were discovered and patronised. New shops were found in the new area, and a new way of life commenced.

So a firm, accustomed over two centuries to moving home, had made the most dramatic change of site in all its long history. Nobody had ever thought of the entire operation moving three miles. The decision had been taken to mark the occasion with a formal opening ceremony, and this took place towards the end of 1970. Aberdeen Journals Ltd. went on show. Both papers and their staffs were determined to demonstrate to their ageing, but still vigorous, proprietor, that his latest investment was a good one.

To preside at the formal opening in December 1970 came Lord Thomson of Fleet. And to perform the official opening ceremony came the Secretary of State for Scotland, Gordon Campbell (afterwards, Lord Campbell of Croy). It was typical of Lord Thomson that, on his way to Mastrick to preside over the large gathering to witness the opening, he looked first at the outside of the Company's old home in Broad Street. He shook his head in disbelief when he saw the antiquated state of the buildings, the congested area and the cramped conditions. 'Did you guys really turn out two daily papers there?' he said, in disbelief.

In the large, new machine hall at Mastrick, the Secretary of State for Scotland unveiled the commemorative plaque, to the applause of the large company which included a goodly number of members of staff, together with representatives of the various unions in the company. Thereafter, at a lunch for 200 people, with the staff liberally represented, Gordon Campbell wished the new enterprise well, and Lord Thomson, in characteristic fashion, offered one of his typically humorous and down to earth speeches. He was loudly cheered by the big company.

For a man in his late seventies, he put in a punishing and demanding day, at the disposal of the Company of which he was chairman. It was a day to be long remembered by everyone participating, and it had been made memorable by the fact that as the Secretary of State unveiled the commemorative plaque, the giant machines in the background roared into life, with a special edition of the *Evening Express* pouring from the folders.

One of his duties earlier that day was to preside over a meeting of the full board of directors of Aberdeen Journals Ltd. of which he was chairman . . . an appointment, he always maintained enthusiastically, that he cherished.

He, and his long-term Scottish associate, James Coltart were joined by the three local directors, K. J. Peters, W. J. Pattillo, formerly the company secretary and chief accountant, and Harry Robertson who had joined the board on his retirement a year earlier. Harry Robertson had been the Company's general circulation manager, and had proved an outstanding executive as well as a capable and popular ambassador for Aberdeen Journals Ltd.—especially in his chairmanship of one of the S.D.N.S. committees. W. P. Forsyth, then secretary of Aberdeen Journals Ltd., completed the board company that historic day.

So, the new headquarters was declared officially open. Twenty months later, a Royal stamp of approval for the enterprise was put firmly and in the most delightful manner by Queen Elizabeth, the Queen Mother.

Despite the ongoing chronicling of the doings of Kings, Queens, Dukes and Princesses in Scotland and the north-east in particular for well over a century by the company's papers, no Royal visitor had ever come to see the staff, its offices and its ceaseless round of activity. Now the Queen Mother arrived, to spend an afternoon at Mastrick, and to encourage and to delight with her enthusiasm and knowledge, all who met her. She was the first Royal visitor in nearly 230 years.

Describing herself in conversation as a long-time reader of the Company's papers, she toured departments and insisted on shaking hands with over 70 people as she walked round.

She talked mutual interests in fishing and gardening with a rapid composing-room enthusiast, Neville Myhill; she discussed industrial relations with the Father of the Federated House Chapel, James Proctor.

Banks of flowers, in colourful bloom, greeted her in the office corridor outside the Board Room. But there was a difference. These magnificent flowers had not been bought just for the occasion. They were supplied by members of the staff who shared with the Queen Mother an intense enthusiasm for horticulture. The staff gardeners really put on a show of shows that late September day in 1972. And their Royal admirer displayed her appreciation of what had been achieved in her honour.

So many people met and spoke with her that day. By common consent throughout the large office, pride of place went to Cuthbert Graham, then Editor of *The Press and Journal*'s Weekend Review and the author, every Saturday, of a special article about an aspect of the north-east countryside. As soon as he began to converse with his Royal reader, it became obvious to him that she was a regular devotee of the columns he wrote and that, in particular, she had read thoroughly his article the previous Saturday.

In honour of the Royal visit to Mastrick, Lord Provost John Smith (afterwards Lord Kirkhill) and the Lady Provost, together with the Chief Constable of Aberdeen, Mr. Alex Morrison, were also the company's guests that afternoon. The official party, with the managing director, his wife and both editors entertained the Queen Mother to tea in the Board Room.

During her stay at Mastrick, the Royal visitor displayed a knowledge of the Company's activities in many fields, especially the work it continued to do with the various charities with which it was involved.

The two papers' link with the little Normandy seaport of St. Valéry-en-Caux, caused by its association with the Army's 51st Highland Division in World War II, came in for her attention. She spoke, of course, as Colonel-in-Chief of one of the famous fighting units which had been involved at St. Valéry in 1940, the Black Watch.

The French people there decided that the growing fund

would be devoted to the establishment and concept of the new Council Chamber in the new Mairie in the town. And it was christened the 'Scottish Room' and officially opened in 1960 when another large civic and military delegation went over to France, with the managing director maintaining Aberdeen Journals' lasting interest and link with the Valeriquais and their kindnesses to the people of north Scotland.

The visit was returned when the Mayor of St. Valéry and his wife paid an official visit to the Highlands and to the north-east and to Aberdeen, at the instigation of *The Press and Journal* and the *Evening Express*.

To mark the 25th anniversary of the liberation of St. Valéry, a further delegation went to the little town in 1969, with Aberdeen Journals Ltd. playing a leading, organising role. Along with the managing director and his wife, who had been members of the 1960 delegation, there went again, to cover the events, the same reporter and photographer as nine years before. Reporter Val Moonie, afterwards assistant news editor of *The Press and Journal* and photographer Ian Hardie, afterwards picture editor, went back on duty, to be warmly received and recognised by the locals.

The St. Valéry link has always been one of the more colourful campaigns sponsored by and helped by Aberdeen Journals Ltd.

With the 51st Division going into captivity there in that fateful summer of 1940, the little seaport had long been in the minds of hundreds of soldiers, themselves prisoners of war until 1945 ... some of whom had actually seen the noted German General Rommel at St. Valéry in 1940. Their relatives, too, knew of the little town which had been shattered by the fierce fighting but parts of which had survived when units of the new '51st' liberated it in the summer of 1944 after the Allies had invaded north-west Europe.

A fund, after the war, had been started by Aberdeen Journals Ltd. to assist with the rebuilding of the town. A granite memorial to the Highland Division was shipped out, at the company's instigation, prior to its unveiling on the cliffs overlooking the town, in 1950. A large party of notable figures in north-east public life attended the ceremony, visited the war graves and provided enthusiastic and personal support in this lovely part of France for the concept of the link between the North of Scotland and St. Valéry.

The man who had, in 1944, led his battalion of Cameron Highlanders to liberate the town, flew from Britain for that 1969 occasion to land at its tiny airstrip. He was by now GOC Scotland and was Lieutenant-General Sir Derek Lang. His imaginative gesture caught the delighted fancy of his French hosts who realised that, as Lieutenant-Colonel Lang, he had been the man to enter St. Valéry that summer of 1944. He had also been captured, during the bitter fighting there, in 1940.

The link survives between the northern part of Scotland and the little French town. Two-way visits by families, schools and private individuals have characterised it and kept flickering the torch. The granite memorial still stands on the cliffs, and the Mayor, as he sits in the chair presented to him by the Highland area cities and towns, can see through his council chamber windows, its grand granite finger pointing skywards. The gate-posts to the British war graves there are of granite, and the Scottish Room in the Mairie contains a number of Scottish gifts donated by well-wishers.

Chapter 18

As the old links were nurtured, and Aberdeen Journals Ltd. occupied its new office in 1970, so men were making exciting discoveries in the North Sea. The oil era had started.

A new and exciting industrial challenge was poised at the doorsteps and harbours of the eastern coast of Scotland. And this challenge more than dispelled any ideas of the north-east of Scotland being a 'cosy corner', as one distinguished British periodical put it.

Life was never to be the same again in the seventies in Aberdeen, and the ports around the north-east coast, as well as Orkney and Shetland. The exploration age for oil had arrived. And, with it, the great companies of this multi-million pound industry.

The harbours of Aberdeen and Montrose and Peterhead were transformed. New, industrial life, of a style, vigour and scope never hitherto dreamed of, came to Orkney and Shetland.

The influx of new and specialised workers to the area, and the arrival of companies with world-famous names, meant new challenges for existing industries, as well as new opportunities.

The Press and Journal and the *Evening Express* found themselves caught up, in an exciting way, with the new era. Added to the ranks of farmers and academics and fishermen, with whom staffs had been in contact, came a new breed of oilmen, developers and explorers. Things moved fast in Aberdeen, which rapidly became the on-shore capital of North Sea oil exploration.

New challenges and new styles were posed for journalists, covering an exciting, new field. New advertising opportunities presented themselves. More copies of both papers had to be printed. The tempo of life in Aberdeen and three miles round quickened appreciably. The Company had moved to Mastrick, it seemed, in the nick of time. The expansion of the activities of both papers, and their staffs, could never have taken place, in the old, antiquated, Broad Street premises. More and more visitors came to our office. People wanted to talk industry, and oil.

Still, however, the distinguished ones came to see the firm. For the first time in many years, the Secretary of State for Scotland was entertained to tea. He was Mr. Willie Ross, who was, in turn, succeeded by Gordon Campbell (afterwards Lord Campbell of Croy) and he had the honour of opening the new plant. Later in the seventies, another Secretary of State, Mr. Bruce Millan, was to visit the Mastrick offices twice within four months, and, after many years of never seeing a cabinet minister, the office basked in the reflected glory of discussions with a Scottish Secretary of State.

In return, as it were, more and more members of the Aberdeen Journals Ltd. executive staff took part in committees and gatherings elsewhere. The Editor of *The Press and Journal*, together with the general circulation manager, and, from time to time, advertisement managers, shared respectively the various sub-committees of the Scottish Daily Newspaper Society. Like his predecessor, K. J. Peters, the managing director, joined the Press Council in the mid-1970s, and was elected to the Board of Directors of Thomson Regional Newspapers. The Company and its papers were quoted more widely. BBC radio news each day included in its summary of the contents of newspapers, extracts from *The Press and Journal*. There was evidence that the influence of the Mastrick firm was growing. Whereas, in many parts of the United Kingdom, towns and cities of Aberdeen's size boasted nowadays only one daily newspaper, Aberdeen maintained its morning and its evening papers, albeit in the face of continual competition from incoming national newspapers, from the competition of rival media, and from the ever-spiralling costs. Nevertheless, as the seventies progressed, it was a source of satisfaction not only to members of the staff but also to the public of the north-east, that the area could still support two daily newspapers.

Much of its papers were widely quoted. The *Evening Express* became well-known for its social conscience, its support of good causes, its sponsoring of an annual and well-loved Christmas carol concert by Aberdeen schoolchildren in the city's Music Hall. It campaigned in depth on a number of fronts, and tackled such with thoroughness and professionalism.

Many regarded one of *The Press and Journal*'s great editorial achievements as the *Weekend Journal*. For the first half of the 1970s, as it had been in the 1960s, this part of *The Press and Journal*, appearing each Saturday, was in the capable, literary hands of Cuthbert Graham, a poet and writer of considerable note. It was interesting for members of the staff to reflect on the fact that Cuthbert Graham followed a long line of other literary figures who had worked for the Company. These ranged from the distinguished novelist Lewis Grassick Gibbon through such capable book reviewers, art, theatre and music critics as W. A. (Sandy) Mitchell, George Rowntree Harvey and the distinguished world-renowned novelist Eric Linklater. Alex Keith, afterwards farmer of note, and George Fraser were other distinguished university graduates who became noted literary columnists in the Company's papers.

Expansion, as inevitably, brought its problems. Even in a brand-new building, the resources of the existing production equipment were stretched to the utmost. Bigger newspapers, more expansion, wider fields of operation by both papers, meant disproportionate strain on the ageing, if honourable, giant presses, type-setting machines, etc.

The staff, as always, was competent and hard-working, typical of the north-east environment. But they were the first to recognise that the continued and welcome expansion of the company's activities could not really be met by the existing machinery and equipment. Important decisions were taken, in 1976, that the composing facilities of Aberdeen Journals Ltd. would gradually be converted from the old, hot metal style to a modern, computer-assisted photocomposition. At the same time, Thomson Regional Newspapers agreed to invest also, on Aberdeen's behalf, in replacement, modern, giant presses to take the place of the honourable veterans, still thundering away nightly and daily, after fifty years of active life.

Officials of the company, and executives of the appropriate composing-room trade union, went to see modern photo-composition in operation. Training schemes were arranged, and operators began their conversion training in 1976 and early 1977, so that the first part of the transition to the modern method of composition began in the spring of 1977. Parts of both papers—mostly advertising, but some of the editorial, also —began to appear using the new method. The first stages on the road to an exciting modernisation plan had thus been taken.

Meanwhile, important staff changes in the senior management team had also taken place. Early in the 1970s, William Forsyth was appointed an assistant managing director, and to replace him as company secretary, the chief accountant, William Jamieson, was appointed. In 1975, James C. Grant, Editor of *The Press and Journal* since 1960, announced his retirement as Editor, and, by a happy coincidence, the award of a C.B.E. to him followed on the succeeding day to the news of his retirement. He remained as the paper's associate editor for the following twelve months.

To edit *The Press and Journal* in his place, Peter Watson, a native of Buckie, was appointed. He had been the paper's deputy editor, and, prior to that, its features editor. Earlier in his career, he had been a member of the communications (wire-room) department, before becoming a journalist, and serving on the *Weekly Journal* and then *The Press and Journal*.

Another long-serving executive of the Company retired in the seventies, Edgar B. Anderson, who had first of all been works manager and then production controller. One of the kenspeckle figures of both Broad Street and Mastrick, and a former machine-man, he had masterminded the production of the Company's newspapers since the death of Alister Sutherland, in the early sixties, when the latter was works manager.

One of Edgar Anderson's great strengths for the company was his ability to train fine subordinates. From time to time, he had in his production management team, assistants or managers who rose to high promotions, both in Aberdeen and elsewhere.

A one-time linotype operator, latterly an assistant and production manager, George H. Dunn afterwards became a production manager at the Thomson Middlesbrough office ... then the production controller of the *Scotsman* and Edinburgh *Evening News*, to establish himself firmly in the mid-seventies as the managing director of Thomson Withy Grove Ltd., a vast publishing office employing over 3,000 people, in Manchester. William Yule, who also left the company's composing-room, to be a manager under Edgar Anderson, had also been one of Aberdeen's project managers for the move from Broad Street to Mastrick. Thereafter he was appointed Middlesbrough's production manager, and, early in 1978, was appointed general manager of Highland Printers Ltd. (the Thomson Group's newspapers at Inverness, Dingwall, Wick and Thurso).

Jack Grayston, the project engineer for the move, was appointed production manager at the Thomson Group's Chester office; Charles Shanks of the tele-communications (wire-room) department joined the production management team, and Forbes D. Singer, of the process engraving department, also joined Edgar Anderson, afterwards to succeed him. The composing-room had not yet completed its supply of potential managers. Raymond Low moved from composing to be, initially, the production manager of *The Press and Journal*, thereafter taking over the *Evening Express*, before moving to Newcastle as chief production manager of the *Newcastle Journal*, *Evening Chronicle* and the *Sunday Sun*. His composing-room colleague, Alexander Thomson became Aberdeen's night production manager, and William Bruce, formerly a composing department trade union official, joined Mr. Singer as his assistant.

Initially, all these executives had been 'spotted' by Edgar Anderson, and many of them encouraged to take their first steps towards executive authority.

Much the same story was told in the accountancy section, where William Forsyth brought in a young accountant, Ernest Petrie, who afterwards joined the London production director's department, before working in Reading and Middlesbrough. Thereafter, he became general manager of Highland Printers

Ltd. at Inverness, before becoming managing director at the Thomson Group's Stockport office. He was still under forty when he was appointed to the latter post. William Jamieson, the company secretary, succeeded in the early autumn of 1978 Roger Nicholson as an assistant managing director when the latter took up a new appointment at Thomson Magazines. Like Petrie, Jamieson was still under forty.

This is a story to which there should be no end . . . at least in the foreseeable future. The *Journal* and the Company to which it gave birth, in its various forms, have seen good times and bad times. As these words are penned, the morning paper's sister publication, the *Evening Express*, is nearing its centenary in 1979.

What the future holds for the two papers, time alone can tell, but it seems safe to assume that, as long as the spirit that animated its pioneer, as long as the principles which governed his approach and that of his successors are maintained, so long will the North of Scotland's papers continue to prosper and to serve generation after generation of readers as they did generation after generation of their forebears. Inspiration gave them birth; inspiration broadened their appeal; and inspiration will, without a doubt, find expression in many new and effective ways in the years that lie ahead.

Index

Abercromby, James, 22
Aberdeen (city): early description of, 10; visited by Burns, 18, 19; visited by Dr. Johnson, 19; Union St. built, 21; union of King's and Marischal Colleges, 31; new Grammar School buildings opened, 32; new Town House opened, 32; Victoria Park laid out, 32; Dee water supply, 56-7; Gallowgate Children's Shelter, 78; Kittybrewster Exhibition Hall, 80-1; Coronation Tattoo, 83; Girder disaster, 78; typhoid outbreak and Queen's visit, 105-8; Mastrick Industrial Estate, 114; and North Sea oil, 122
Aberdeen, Countess of (Ishbel), 40-1
Aberdeen, 7th Earl of, later 1st Marquess of A. and Temair (John Campbell Gordon), 30
Aberdeen, 2nd Marquess of (George Gordon), 5, 87-8
Aberdeen Almanack, 19, 20
Aberdeen and North of Scotland Newspaper and Printing Co. Ltd.: is set up, 34-7; publishes *Aberdeen Journal* as daily, 36, 37; liquidation and reconstitution of, 42; makes profit, 43; and local Conservatives, 44; and bids from Liberals and *Aber-*

deen Free Press, 44; and legacy of J. G. Chalmers, 45; moves to Broad St., 46; increases profit, 48; buys Linotype machines, 48; appoints Coutts Manager, 49; pays Directors, 50; solves delivery problems, 51; issues dividends, 51, 54, 55; 21st anniversary, 55; and adjacent properties, 56, 58; cooperation and amalgamation with *Aberdeen Free Press*, 59, 60-1; liquidates and sells assets to Aberdeen Newspapers Ltd., 61
Aberdeen Association of Social Services, 110
Aberdeen Banner, 27
Aberdeen Chronicle, 25
Aberdeen Constitutional, 27
Aberdeen Daily Free Press see *Aberdeen Free Press*
Aberdeen Directory, 20
Aberdeen Free Press: launched, 27; and Carnie, 62; becomes a daily, 62; M'Combie and Alexander as Editors, 62; rivalry with *Aberdeen Journal*, 27, 34; on Dee-Avon dispute, 57; and World War I, 59; politics of, 62-3; is helped by and amalgamates with *Aberdeen Journal*, 60, 61; mentioned, 54, 67

Aberdeen Weekly Journal, 85, 90, 91-2, 125
Aberdeen's Journal and North British Magazine, 1, 9-12
Adam, James, 26, 28
advertisements and advertising: early, 9, 12, 13; *Aberdeen Journal*'s lead in, 27; on tram tickets, 50; mentioned, 48, 59, 85, 91, 100, 108, 109, 111
Alexander, Henry, 61, 67, 68
Alexander, William, 65
Alexander, Dr. William McCombie, 61-2
Allied Newspapers Ltd. (later Kemsley Newspapers Ltd., q.v.), 72, 73, 74, 77
Anderson, Edgar B., 125, 126
Anderson, Robert (Editor of *Aberdeen Journal*), 54
Anderson, Robert (Editor of *Evening Express*), 90, 93

Balmer, Thomas, 36
Balmoral Castle, 31, 49
Barclay, Mr. (of Knockleith), 28
Bawden, H. R., 93, 97
B.B.C. press review, 123
Berry, James Gomer (1st Viscount Kemsley), 72-3, 77, 87-8, 94, 95, 99
Berry, Hon. Lionel (2nd Viscount Kemsley), 87
Berry, Hon. Pamela (Marchioness of Huntly), 77, 79, 87, 89, 95
Berry, William Ewert (1st Viscount Camrose), 72-3
Bird, Peter, 47, 103
Bisset, Rev. John, 2
Black Watch, The (Royal Highland Regiment), 119
Blackwood's Magazine, 29
Boer War (1899-1902), 51, 77
Boswell, James, 19
British Council, Scottish Advisory

Committee of, 109
Brown, Robert, 28
Bruce, John, 61
Bruce, Sir Robert, 47, 62, 65, 68
Bruce William, 126
Buchan, John Norman Stuart (2nd Baron Tweedsmuir), 20
Burn, Col., 55
Burns, Robert, 18-19, 20
Business and Professional Club, 110

Caithness, 16th Earl of (James Augustus Sinclair), 37, 42, 45
Cameron Highlanders, 121
Campbell, Gordon (Baron Campbell of Croy), 117, 123
Camrose, 1st Viscount (William Ewert Berry), 72-3
Carnie, William, 62
Catto, Alexander, 58, 71
Chalmers, C. & P. H., 35, 42, 73
Chalmers, D. M. A. ('Monty'), 22, 42, 43, 44, 46, 73
Chalmers, David (grandson of founder), 22, 25-8, 30-1, 42
Chalmers, James (founder of *Aberdeen Journal*): sets up press, 4; and Jacobites, 1-2; in army, 3, 4, 5; and Culloden broadsheet, 3-4; and No. 1 edition of *The Aberdeen's Journal*, 9-12; his New Year messages, 15; and *Aberdeen Intelligencer*, 16; charged with false representation, 16-17; and Alexander Cruden, 48; mentioned, 18, 29, 31, 88
Chalmers, James (the 'Second'): succeeds father, 18; and Burns and Bishop Skinner, 18-19; other publications of, 20; and grandfather clock, 22; and Eagle proofing press and Waterloo bulletin, 22-4

'new look', 92; Bawden succeeds Anderson as Editor, 93; and Thomson take-over, 94; Robert Smith as Editor, 97; and typhoid outbreak, 106; link with St. Valéry, 119-21; special edition for Mastrick opening, 118; and North Sea oil, 122; and introduction of computer-assisted photocomposition, 124-5; circulation figures, 27, 59, 91, 94; approaches centenary, 127
Evening Gazette, 58, 61
Evening Worlds, 72
exhibitions, 80-1, 105

Fennell, David, 111
Ferguson, William, of Kinmundy, 36
Ferguson, William Black, 36
51st (Highland) Division, 79, 89, 101, 119, 120
Films of Scotland Committee, 110
Fleming, Ian, 73
folio numbers, 5, 37
Forbes, J., 47
Fordyce, Dingwall, 34
Forestry Commission, 89
Forsyth, William, 30, 36, 38-9, 49
Forsyth, William P., 97, 101, 103, 118, 125, 126
Fraser, George, 85, 124
Fraser, R., 47
Frederick Snowdon, 78
freedom of the Press, 15

Gall, John, 47
Gallowgate Children's Shelter, 78
Gazette, 58, 61
Gemmell, A., 47
General Strike, 68-9, 70
George III, 52
George IV, 52

George V, 82
George VI, 31, 82, 87
'Gibbon, Lewis Grassic' (James Leslie Mitchell), 75, 124
Giles, James, 29
Gillies, William, 37, 38, 39, 41, 42, 44, 46
Girder Disaster Trust Fund, 78, 97, 109
Gladstonian Party, 44; *see also* Liberals and Liberal Party
Glasgow Herald, 26, 27, 28, 47, 57
Gordon, George (2nd Marquess of Aberdeen), 5, 87-8
Gordon, John Campbell (7th Earl of Aberdeen, later 1st Marquess of A. and Temair), 30
Gordon Highlanders, 83
Graham, Cuthbert, 85, 119, 124
Graham, Rev. Prof. John, Lord Provost, 114
Grampian Television Ltd., 108, 109
Grant, James C., 97, 125
Gray, Mr. (chief sub-editor of *Aberdeen Journal*), 42
Grayston, Jack, 126
Great North of Scotland Railway, 31

Hamilton, Denis, 101
Hardie, Ian, 120
Harmsworth, Harold Sydney (1st Viscount Rothermere), 72
Harvey, George Rowntree, 88, 124
Hay, John A. M., 74
Henderson, J., 47
Henderson, John M. & Co., 90
Highland Printers Ltd., 126
His Majesty's Theatre, 93, 108
Hoe printing-machine, 44, 48
Hogg, Norman, Lord Provost, 106, 107

Noble, John, 97
North of Scotland Gazette, 62
North Sea oil, 122-3
North Star, 34
Northcliffe Newspapers Ltd., 72, 74
Northern Gazette and Literary Chronicle and Review of the Month, 20
Northern Industries, 80
Northern News, 46
Northern Newspaper Co., 46

Ogg, William, 49, 50, 75, 98
Ogilvie, John, 70

Pattillo, William J., 97, 98, 118
Pearey, W. H., 101
Penny Free Press, 62
Perth Advertiser, 27
Peters, Kenneth J., 90, 95, 97, 98, 109, 118
Peters, William J., 68
Petrie, Ernest, 126
Pettigrew, J. R., 58-9
Pratt, Geoffrey, 100-1
Press, freedom of, 15
Press and Journal: beginnings of, 61-2; accommodation problems, 65-6; London office, 65, 67, 68; generator installed, 67; Strike editions of, 68-9; Maxwell resigns, 70; Veitch as Editor-in-Chief, 71; under Allied Newspapers Ltd., 73, 77; and relief funds, 77-8; finances travelling scholarships, 79-80; organises exhibitions, 80-1; and events of 1936, 82; sponsors Coronation Tattoo, 83; and World War II, 84; J. M. Chalmers as Editor, 85; Saturday Review of, 86; bicentenary of, 3, 5, 87; and 51st (Highland) Div. Monument and St. Valéry,

79, 119-21; George E. Ley Smith as Editor, 88; and Great Gale of 1953, 89; and Coronation of Elizabeth II, 89-90; retirement of Veitch, 91; taken over by Thomson, 94; Grant succeeds K. J. Peters as Editor, 97; and typhoid outbreak, 106-107; and other dailies, 108; produced from Mastrick, 116; and North Sea oil, 122; staff serve on outside bodies, 123; and *Weekend Journal*, 124; computer-assisted photocomposition introduced, 124-5; Watson as Editor, 125; other staff changes, 126
Press Council, The, 91, 110, 123
Pressly, David, 47, 49, 54
Pretoria, relief of (1900), 51
printing machines, 22-4, 28, 42, 44, 48
Pritchard, Roy, 111
Proctor, James, 119
public relations, 80-1, 100, 101, 105

Ramsay, John, 28-30
Ramsden, Denis, 93
Reid, Walter A., 45
relief funds, 77-9, 97, 109
repeal of Stamp Act (1855), 27, 62
Roberts, 1st Earl (Gen. Frederick Sleigh Roberts), 40, 51
Robertson, Harry, 98, 118
Robertson, Joseph, 28
Ross, Dallas, 41
Ross, Edward, 35
Ross, Rt. Hon. William, 123
Rothermere, 1st Viscount (Harold Sydney Harmsworth), 72
Russell, Alexander, 63

St. Nicholas Church, 21, 30, 34

Watson, Peter, 125
Watt, Edward William, 62, 65, 68
Watt, J., 47
Watts, House of, 4
Webster Bros., 51
Weekend Journal, 124
Weekend Review (of *Press and Journal*), 119
Weekly Journal, 85, 90, 91–2, 125
Weir, Mr., leader-writer, 28
Whatmore Players, 93
William IV, 52

Williamson, James, 106, 107
Willing Shilling Fund, 78
Wistow Hall, 78
Wolrige-Gordon, Henry, 36
Wood, R., 47
World War I (1914–1918), 59–60
World War II (1939–1945), 8, 78, 79, 84–5, 88, 97, 119
W.V.S., 78

Yeats, William, 36, 38
Yule, William, 126